UTERINE DISEASES,

WITH AN APPENDIX,

CONTAINING AN

ABSTRACT OF 180 CASES

OF

UTERINE DISEASES AND THEIR TREATMENT,

TOGETHER WITH

ANALYTICAL TABLES OF RESULTS, AGES, SYMPTOMS, ETC.,

TO WHICH IS ADDED

A CLINICAL RECORD OF INTERESTING CASES, TREATED IN THE MANCHESTER HOMŒOPATHIC HOSPITAL.

BY HENRY R. MADDEN, M. D.

NEW-YORK:
WILLIAM RADDE, 322 BROADWAY.
PHILADELPHIA: RADEMACHER & SHEEK.—BOSTON: OTIS CLAPP.—ST. LOUIS: C. F. WESSELHOEFT.—CINCINNATI: H. F. DAVIS, M.D.

UTERINE DISEASES,

WITH AN APPENDIX,

CONTAINING AN

ABSTRACT OF 180 CASES

OF

UTERINE DISEASES AND THEIR TREATMENT,

TOGETHER WITH

ANALYTICAL TABLES OF RESULTS, AGES, SYMPTOMS, ETC.,

TO WHICH IS ADDED

A CLINICAL RECORD OF INTERESTING CASES, TREATED IN THE MANCHESTER HOMŒOPATHIC HOSPITAL.

BY HENRY R. MADDEN, M. D.

NEW-YORK:
WILLIAM RADDE, 322 BROADWAY.
PHILADELPHIA: RADEMACHER & SHEEK.—BOSTON: OTIS CLAPP.—ST. LOUIS: C. F. WESSELHOEFT.—CINCINNATI: H. F. DAVIS, M.D.

ANGELL, ENGEL & HEWITT,
Printers,
1, 3 and 5 Spruce-st., N. Y.

UTERINE DISEASES.

THERE is perhaps no class of diseases concerning which the views of the profession have undergone so complete a revolution, within a comparatively short period, as that to which I am now about to draw your attention. Prior to the appearance of the well known work, "On the Diseases of Females which are attended by Discharges," from the pen of Sir Charles Clarke, in the year 1814, the medical men of Great Britain appear to have been in almost mid-night darkness respecting the true nature of this most common source of delicacy among females; and subsequent to the advance in knowledge attributable to the above work, but little real progress appears to have been made until about 1843, when Professor Simpson startled the profession by his bold advances upon the almost untrodden field of uterine diagnosis.—It may be well to observe *en passant* that these remarks refer only to Britain, since the advancement in the knowledge of uterine pathology in France has been far more steady and progressive for many years past.—Since the appointment of the present Midwifery Professor of Edinburgh however, a most complete change has occurred in the feelings of the profession towards this field of research. The stimulus given at our Scottish University has excited a deep and lasting interest in the whole subject, and has encouraged, or called into active exercise, so many ardent minds that we now seem likely to suffer from an evil the very opposite of that which characterized the last generation of practitioners; and every aberration of health in the female sex runs no small risk of being at once attributed to 'uterine engorgement,' 'inflammation of the cervix,' 'retroversion,' or some other metritic malady, the very mention of which has a 'harrowing interest' for the poor sufferer. This however is an evil which may be avoided by due care and circumspection; and we cannot feel otherwise than grateful to those who have directed our special attention to this most interesting class of diseases, and who have led the way into an entirely new field of pathological enquiry. On viewing, however, what has hitherto been done, the cautious and the wary cannot avoid feeling, that while some advance has been already made, much more yet remains to be achieved; and while some solid foundation has been laid whereupon to rear a useful and practical pathology, a careful examination of the superstructure will excite some doubt as to its stability and endurance. Time will not permit me to dwell any longer upon such general remarks, and I must, accordingly, advance without further delay to the consideration of the subject itself.

To any one who has read much of the recent literature of uterine disease, it will at once be apparent that any attempt to touch, even in the most sketchy and superficial manner, upon all the various points of this wide-branching subject, would occupy vastly more time than can possibly be commanded on an occasion like the present. It is, accordingly, my purpose to limit the following remarks almost exclusively to one portion of this subject, which, however, is of itself so extensive and important as well to merit all the attention and time we can devote to it. I shall therefore, at once, draw your attention to the consideration of

Subacute and Chronic Inflammation of the Uterine Tissues, and still further to limit our subject, I shall confine my observations chiefly to the disease in its most common form, namely, as affecting chiefly the cervix uteri, and as limited to the mucous membrane of that portion of the genital apparatus. Although in the remarks with which I opened up this subject, I referred to Professor Simpson as the individual to whose labours I would trace the extraordinary stimulus given to the study of this class of diseases in Britain, yet it will appear from the sequel that Dr. Henry Bennet, of London, has done more than any other practitioner in this country to advance our knowledge of that special form of disease which we are now considering.

It will facilitate greatly our examination of this subject, if I, in the first place, give a short and rapid sketch of the views which have been progressively advanced regarding this disease during the last seven years. It was in 1843 that Professor Simpson first publicly introduced to the notice of the profession that instrument of diagnosis, which is now so well known by the name of the Uterine Sound; and he, at the same time, informed his confrères that he had proved, by its means, that flexures of the uterus, in place of being conditions of rare occurrence, were among the most frequent accompaniments of uterine derangement. Nay, more, he believed himself authorized in affirming, that these flexures were the cause of very much, if not of all, the distressing symptoms under which such patients suffered; and yet further, he added, that these morbid conditions admitted of a mechanical cure, subsequent to which the whole symptoms yielded, and the patient was restored to health. To this statement we may trace the origin of what may not inaptly be termed the "Mechanical School" of uterine therapeutics. This school has grown largely in numbers since the enunciation of the above related facts, and counts among its advocates many of the leading accoucheurs of this country. It has, however, been vigorously opposed by a large number of those who have made uterine pathology their chief study. Neither has this opposition been solely on the part of the conservative section of our profession—whose peculiar prerogative it seems to be, to exert all their efforts for the purpose of impeding progress, or, as they would themselves say, of putting a wholesome curb on reckless innovation–but an equally energetic resistance to the adoption of these mechanical views has been made by some of the most ardent reformers of uterine pathology, and who, themselves occupying a position quite as far in advance of the mass of the profession as the Edinburgh professor and his pupils, share equally with them the opprobrium of those whose affections are placed upon things as they are.

The leaders of this second, or Inflammatory School, as it might be termed, is Dr. Henry Bennet, of London, who, after studying his subject fully in Paris, has developed his views in the very best book of uterine diseases extant in this country, I mean his work on "Inflammation of the Uterus and its Appendages," published in 1849.

Dr. Bennet and his followers, unlike the conservative section of the profession, freely acknowledge the importance of the uterine sound as a most useful, nay, often indispensable, means of diagnosis, while they altogether differ from Dr. Simpson in their estimate of the importance of those frequently occurring flexures of the organ, which have become known to the profession through its instrumentality; and so far from viewing them as the chief object of treatment, they aver that if the inflammatory condition of the uterus be subdued, no attention whatever need be paid to the bent state of the organ, save in rare exceptional cases. This opinion they support by the declaration, that when the flexure is slight it rights itself as the organ resumes its healthy condition; while, on the other hand, if the flexure is not unbent, but remains stationary, it ceases to cause any inconvenience once the inflammation is entirely subdued. We have here, therefore, another of those frequent instances of a disease, wherein the most opposite opinions are held and acted upon by different practitioners, and yet the followers of both methods of treatment, meet with a sufficient amount of success to encourage them to persevere with the plan they have adopted, and uphold the accuracy of the opinions they have propounded respecting the nature of the disease and its therapeutic requirements. In what way are we to explain this apparent anomaly? Are we to consider it as a proof that neither method of treatment does any real good? or, should we not rather examine the whole question more closely, and see whether the two methods of treatment do, in their essence, differ as much from each other as they at first sight appear to do; and whether a rational explanation of their action may not be found, which will equally account for the success of both? This, however, will be more conveniently considered when we are engaged with the whole question of treatment.

I will now endeavour to lay before you the various points which it appears to me have been, more or less, positively established by recent investigators of uterine pathology, irrespective altogether of the school to which the propounders may belong; for in this, as in most other instances, a careful and dispassionate consideration of the statements made by each party has led me to see that both contain much that is valuable, and that the safest plan is to keep clear of parties altogether, and endeavour to reap the benefits rendered available by the labours of each and all of those engaged in the investigation.

Perhaps one of the most important facts, in a practical point of view, which has been established, is that leucorrhœa is an invariable proof of an inflammatory condition of some part of the uterine system. The converse of this is not indeed true, in so far as inflammation of the uterus or its appendages is by no means invariably accompanied by leucorrhœa; but, on the other hand, it appears to have been clearly demonstrated that in every case of continued leucorrhœa, there exists more or less inflammation of one or other of the uterine tissues. It is curious, but not uninstructive, to notice the reception which the declaration of the inflammatory origin of leucorrhœa met with in this country. The first announcement of this doctrine in later years which I have met with, is by M. Lisfranc, in his *Clinique Chirurgicale*, published in 1842, and reviewed in the *Medico-Chirurgical Review* for April, 1843. In that periodical we find the following remarks (p. 366–7):—

"*Leucorrhœa.*—The following most *lucid* exposition of the ætiology of this very common complaint is given by M. Lisfranc:—'This disease is produced either by a phlegmasia, or by an irritation, or by an injection, or, perhaps, by a sanguineous fluxion, which may exist at one and the same time, in the vulva, the vagina, the internal surface of the uterus, and the ovarian tubes, whence arises a white coloured discharge.' We verily believe that, for once that it is owing to any increased vascular action—be the name that we give to such a state what it may—it is in nineteen, or ninety-nine cases, at least, dependent upon weakness and atony of the vessels of the mucous membrane affected."

And a little further on, the reviewer winds up his remarks by observing—

"But it is unnecessary to address arguments to the English physician on this subject, as very few are likely to be misled by the fantastic notions of many continental writers."

Such, then, is the opinion of an influential review, in 1843, concerning the inflammatory nature of leucorrhœa. But what says the same Review, or, rather, its successor, the *British and Foreign Medico-Chirurgical Review*, in 1850? In speaking of Dr. Bennet's work on "Inflammation of the Uterus and its Appendages," we find at page 115, the following remarks:—

"Among the disorders of the female constitution, there is none so frequent, none so much misunderstood as leucorrhœa. Its name implies nothing more than an effect of some pre-existing disease. The cause of that effect should be enquired into and understood, before we undertake its removal; yet the treatment formerly adopted, almost exclusively consisted in remedies to check the discharge; every variety of astringent was used for this sole purpose; and whether administered by the mouth, and taken into the circulation, or applied locally, the whole object was to arrest the fluor albus, and nothing more."

After referring to the one step in advance, made by Sir Chas. Clarke, the reviewer proceeds—

"Such was the state of our ignorance on this class of diseases, until within the last few years;—an ignorance which was not the result of a careless attention to them, or of want of acuteness on the part of the obstetric physician, but which was inevitable so long as the mode of ascertaining their character was not adequate for the purpose."

Further on, in the same article, we meet with the following sentence (p. 132)—

"Practitioners have considered these symptoms as purely functional; and although often embarrassed to explain their anomalous character, or to decide exactly upon the function that was disordered, a local phlegmasia was the very last cause that would have been looked for to unravel our entangled ideas."

Nevertheless, it appears obvious from the whole tenor of the article, that the doctrine of the inflammatory origin of leucorrhœa commends itself to the judgment of the reviewer; and in the July number of the same periodical, in treating of Dr. Tilt's work on the "Diseases of Menstruation," we find, apparently the same writer, remarking that the term leucorrhœa

"Must for the future have a precise meaning, and be regarded almost entirely as symptomatic of well-recognised organic disease."—(p. 212.)

Thus, it appears, that the "fantastic notions" which "are not likely to mislead" the English physician in 1843, become acknowledged truths in 1850. How passing strange, that a learned profession like that of medicine, should be acting and re-acting the same farce of ridicule and concession, of disparagement and adoption, of incredulity and faith, respecting almost every new fact which may be presented to its notice!

Let us examine, however, the ground upon which this opinion, respecting the inflammatory origin of leucorrhœa, rests. This we find to be two-fold, viz., *experimental* and *deductive.*

Experimentally, it has been *proved* by examination of the uterus. *Deductively*, the results of such examinations have been brought to bear upon certain cases, evincing similar symptoms, but where no opportunity for examination was afforded, or where there appeared no paramount necessity for the performance of an operation which must ever be far from agreeable to the feelings both of the physician and his patient.

It is perfectly obvious, that the true nature of leucorrhœa would have ever remained undiscovered had not the speculum been extensively resorted to for its elucidation. Sir Charles Clarke had already pointed out to the profession the importance of a physical examination of the condition of the generative apparatus in all cases of leucorrhœa; but he limited his investigations to the data afforded by the sense of touch, and the profession soon found, that the information thus obtained assisted them very little more in their treatment than the symptoms which were related to them by the patient, and thus, except in aggravated or very obstinate cases, this mode of investigation was employed only by a few of those who more especially devoted their attention to female diseases; and, as a consequence, but little real advance was made, either in the knowledge or treatment of this most common ailment. When, however, the speculum came into general use, first in Paris, and subsequently in this country, and an opportunity was thus afforded for carrying out the physical examination of the uterus to a much fuller extent, it was very soon ascertained, that the cervix and cervical canal, in all cases of leucorrhœa, presented, to a greater or less degree, certain alterations and morbid conditions which obviously indicated the existence of inflammation. It would be impossible, without altogether overstepping the ordinary bounds of a paper like the present, for me to enter fully into a description of the natural condition of these parts, as ascertained by the speculum, and the alterations and modifications which they undergo, when affected with inflammation; still less will it be possible to show the grounds upon which Dr. Bennet bases his opinion, which limits the disease, in the majority of such cases, to the mucous membrane of the cervix. Nevertheless, I may briefly lay before you the results of Dr. Bennet's investigations, and more especially those which I have had opportunities of fully verifying in practice.

If a female, labouring under leucorrhœa, or even decided menstrual derangement, such as dysmenorrhœa, menorrhagia,

&c., be examined by the speculum, one or other of the following appearances will be detected.

1. The cervix uteri may appear perfectly normal, smooth, and unctuous, and of its healthy pale flesh colour, and the os may be smooth and circular, but the cervical canal will be seen filled with a transparent glairy fluid, which is removed with difficulty, by a piece of lint or sponge, and which is so viscid as to draw out into long threads; and, if this secretion be carefully removed, and the lips of the os uteri carefully separated, the lining membrane of the canal will be seen of a bright red colour, very much deeper than the surrounding mucous membrane of the cervix, and resembling greatly the appearance of a pretty large bronchial tube, in a case of acute bronchitis. If the uterine sound be passed along the canal, it frequently, though by no means always, causes considerable pain, and is still more frequently followed by an oozing of blood from the inflamed membrane. This is the mildest form of the disease, and may be termed the first stage of *cervico-metritis*, by which name we can distinguish the disease when confined to the neck of the uterus, from the general disease of *chronic metritis* with which it is ordinarily confounded.

2. One step in advance of this, at least as regards the severity of the pathological modifications of the part, is when the os uteri is dilated, and more or less transverse, or oval in place of circular: this change varying from a slightly oval form of aperture, to that of an irregular gaping slit. In this case, the lining membrane of the cervical canal is generally found to be more or less excoriated, and the inflammatory redness extends beyond the orifice, and spreads slightly over the lips of the cervix; the secretion, in such a case, may be entirely of the glairy character above described, but it is more frequently either milky or, to a greater or less extent, mingled with muco-pus. The dilatation of the cervical canal, in these cases, is a symptom of great importance, since Dr. Bennet has brought forward numerous arguments to prove that the extent of this dilatation marks accurately the extent of the inflammation,

that is to say, when the dilatation only extends part of the way up the cervical canal, we may conclude, that to this extent only has the inflammation advanced. Or, again: if the dilatation only reaches to the *os uteri internum*, leaving the co-arctation at this point in its normal condition, we may then conclude that the disease is limited to the canal of the cervix, and that the interior of the uterus remains unaffected.

3. Ulceration, more or less extensive, of the lips of the uterus constitutes a third stage in the severity of this disease. In strict language, it would, perhaps, be better to call these "granulated abrasions" than ulcers, seeing that they seldom present any excavation, and but rarely do the granulations project above the general level of the surface. Uterine pathologists have spoken of several different kinds of ulcer as occurring in this region, but, for practical purposes, three varieties only require to be noticed, viz., the *simple*, which I have just described; the *syphilitic*, which, according to Dr. Bennet, is of much rarer occurrence than is generally supposed; and the *phagedenic*, which is a much graver disease, is of by no means frequent occurrence, and is most usually associated with cancer, or some other malignant disease of the uterine tissues. These two latter varieties will not be examined or discussed in the present paper.

4. A fourth stage of severity may be noted, when, in consequence of the inflammation affecting the deeper tissues of the uterine neck, there has occurred more or less extensive infiltration into the cellular tissue, and consequent enlargement of this organ, giving rise to induration and irregularity of the cervix, which may or may not be accompanied by ulceration. This induration has often led medical men to give a very unfavourable prognosis of a case, and to suspect the existence of schirrus; it is of great importance, therefore, that we should bear in mind the characteristics by which simple inflammatory induration may be distinguished from the graver malady. Dr. Bennet describes these very well, in the first edition of his work on

"Uterine Inflammation." He remarks at p. 129, speaking of Cancer:—

"In the first stage of the disease, the uterine neck becomes very hard, the indurated tissue being irregular in its surface, lobulated, presenting shot-like tubercles. It is not, however, the hardness of the diseased cervix which indicates the invasion of cancer, for, as we have seen, cases of non-malignant inflammation may be followed by stony hardness of the organ, or a part of it, but the *irregularity* of the hardened surface, and the existence of tubercles, which project here and there."

It must not be supposed, however, that every irregularity of the indurated portions is a proof of the cancerous character of the affection, for, on the contrary, when this disease occurs, as it very frequently does, in women who have had large families, we very often find the surface of the uterine neck irregular and lobulated, and some of the lobules may be indurated to a degree of hardness almost, if not quite, equal to that existing in the first stage of cancer. A careful examination of such a case, however, will show that while the diseased part, considered as a whole, is, indeed, lobulated, or rather divided into segments by fissures, *each lobule is smooth and regular*, and there are none of those characteristic tubercles projecting from its surface to which Dr. Bennet refers.

Another important point to notice is, that since the fissures, in the non-malignant disease, are invariably the fissures so well-known to accoucheurs, as occurring after severe labours or miscarriages, and which always radiate from the os uteri towards the exterior of the labia uteri, so in these cases "the fissures which separate the lobes radiate round the cavity of the os as a centre, which is not the case in cancerous tumours."—(*Bennet*, 1*st edit. p.* 130.)

5. Hitherto I have been describing the disease as confined to the cervix uteri and its canal; unfortunately, however, both for the patient and the physician, this is by no means always the case; for while I feel disposed, in a great measure, to agree with Dr. Bennet in his views, respecting the infinitely greater

frequency of inflammation of the mucous membrane of the cervical canal, than of true *endo-metritis*, it is most obvious that chronic metritis, especially as affecting certain portions only of the body of the uterus, is a disease of extreme frequency, and proves the cause of much discomfort and functional distress to the patient.

In discussing this subject, I feel that I must, of necessity, pass over much which might be interesting and not without its value, but the necessity for keeping my remarks within convenient limits will render such a course imperative. I shall accordingly confine myself almost entirely to the development of the results which have been arrived at by myself and various investigators, without detailing the controversial process through which each of these results has passed ere it could be admitted as proved, or even rendered highly probable.

When the uterus becomes congested, it of course increases in bulk and weight, and being a floating organ, it sinks down more or less, into the pelvis. The mobility of this organ is vastly greater than one would suppose; thus M. Lisfranc states, that it can descend one or two inches in the act of defecation, and I have myself little doubt but his statement is correct. When the uterus descends in the pelvis, as for example, at each successive menstrual period, and still more at the commencement of pregnancy, it follows the well known curvilinear direction of the pelvic axis, and in so doing it does not exercise any unequal pressure upon the surrounding organs, and accordingly unless the descent, or prolapsus, is to a considerable extent, it causes little or no discomfort to the patient beyond a sense of weight. In order, however, that the uterus should thus descend in the direct line of the pelvic axis, it is obvious that its increase of bulk and weight must be perfectly uniform—because, as it is a floating organ, and can move in many other directions, as well as downwards, it follows, that if the increase of bulk be partial, the position of the centre of gravity of the whole organ will be altered, and in falling downwards it will also fall either forwards, backwards, or towards one side, according to the direction of the preponderating weight.

This accordingly happens in a large proportion of cases, owing to the fact, now distinctly proved, that the uterus is more frequently affected with partial than general metritis, and that, in consequence, one or other of its walls becomes proportionably the heavier. Of the two walls it is generally supposed that the posterior is the more frequently affected, and certainly my experience would go to corroborate this; nevertheless the more extended experience of Professor Simpson would lead to the conclusion, that the affections of the two walls are almost equally common, since he speaks of antiversion of the uterus being "almost equally common" with retroversion, and these conditions are, I believe, capable of being demonstrated as the results of partial inflammation and subsequent enlargement of the uterus.

Bearing in mind what I have already said respecting the influence of irregular enlargement on the position of the uterus when descending from its increased weight, let us follow the progress of a uterus wherein the posterior wall has become enlarged, owing to chronic metritis. The uterus, in this instance,

Fig. 1. Fig. 2. Fig. 3.

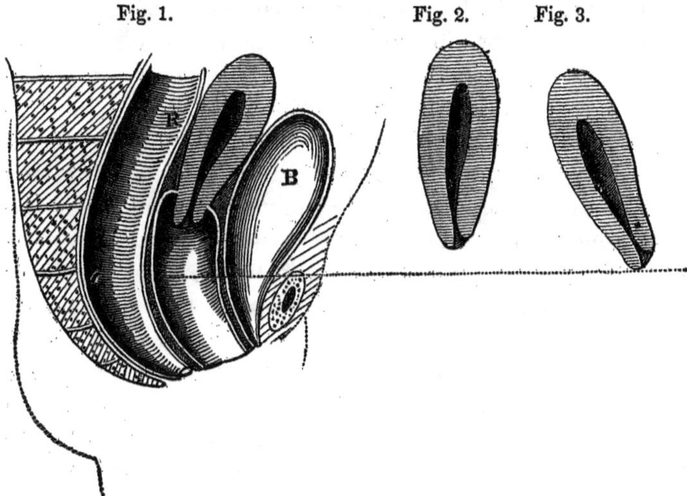

will not follow the direct axis of the pelvis, but will be tilted backwards, and thus assume the form represented in figure 4 of the accompanying diagram—its fundus pressing against the rectum, and the cervix tilted forwards in the direction of the pubis. Matters, however, do not long remain in this position, for the fundus now pressing and causing mechanical contraction of the calibre of the rectum, an obstacle is offered to the descent of the fæces, which accordingly accumulate to a certain extent above the obstruction, and then, when carried forward, have a tendency to carry the uterus along with them; and this process being continually repeated, the uterus gradually assumes the mal-position figured in Nos. 5 and 6 of the diagram, and which

Fig. 4. Fig. 5. Fig. 6.

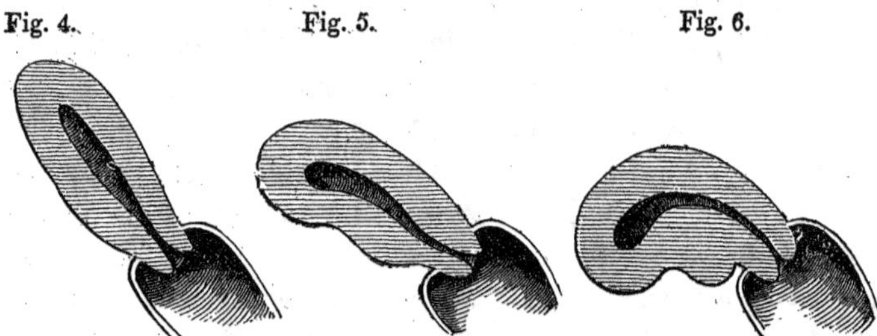

constitute different degrees of well marked retroflexion. On examining these two figures, you will observe one or two circumstances well deserving of attention: for example, in figure 6, the finger passed along the posterior wall of the vagina, will not detect the fundus uteri, but will come in contact with the engorged part of the posterior wall, and will feel this, projecting like a knuckle, immediately behind the point where the mucous membrane of the cervix is reflected on to the posterior wall of the vagina—and this projection will be found very tender to the touch in many cases. This projection has been repeatedly mistaken for tumour, pelvic abscess, &c., and, more recently, by some of the followers of Dr. Simpson, for the fundus. A careful examination, however, with the uterine sound, reveals its true nature; for if the finger be kept in contact with it, and the sound be introduced, it will be found to pass over, without entering, this projection; and when the uterus is replaced in its normal position, by revolving the sound, this projection is carried forwards and upwards, and by the stretching of the posterior wall, consequent on the re-adjustment, it, in many cases, altogether disappears. In cases where the retroversion is greater than at Fig. 6, however, the fundus uteri can be distinctly felt through the posterior wall of the vagina, and on examining with the sound, the instrument is felt to enter the tumour, which, in its turn, entirely disappears, when the instrument is turned round.

In the case of the anterior wall being engorged, an opposite series of changes are set on foot, but owing to the much greater elasticity and pliability of the cervix, which is the part that in this case presses against the rectum, and owing to the steady support afforded to the fundus when tilted forwards by the bladder and its ligaments, we much less frequently meet with cases of antiversion where the flexure of the organ is by any means so great as that which accompanies the bending of the organ backwards.

Such I believe to be the series of changes which occur in consequence of partial engorgement of the uterus, owing to the existence of chronic metritis; and it is in this manner, I believe, that the very common flexures of this organ, which the uterine sound has revealed to us, are produced. I am well aware that other and very different explanations of the cause and manner of production of these flexures have been brought before the profession, but no explanation which I have met with, except the preceding, appears to harmonize with all the facts revealed to us by practice. Thus, Mr. Joseph Bell, of Glasgow, in an excellent and ingenious paper, on the displacements of the unimpregnated uterus, which appeared in the *Monthly Journal of Medical Sciences* for September, 1848, after speaking of congestion and enlargement of the uterus giving rise to displacement, asserts that if either wall of the uterus be hypertrophied or atrophied, curvature must occur, since the largest wall must also be the *longest*, and the two being united together the longer will, of necessity, become convex. The great objection to this proposition, however, is the undeniable fact, that in retroversion the posterior wall is felt to be enlarged and tender, whereas, according to Mr. Bell's theory, it should be either healthy or atrophied. Again: Professor Simpson remarks, in his essay on "Retroversion," which appeared in the *Dublin Quarterly Journal of Medical Science* for May, 1848, that—"in a large proportion of cases, the retroverted uterus is in no degree enlarged or increased in volume, but natural in size." Now, while there are certainly many cases in which the normal length of the uterine cavity is not increased, yet, in a very large number of such cases, we find tenderness and other symptoms of engorgement of the posterior wall, and all experience tells us that where there is engorgement there is, at the same time, increase of bulk and weight. Moreover, in chronic cases it is perfectly conceivable that the organ, once fully bent, should retain its abnormal position even after all trace of engorgement has disappeared.

Before quitting the subject of uterine flexures, I must guard those who make use of the sound against a by no means unfrequent cause of error in diagnosis, whereby retroversion is apt to be made out a much more frequent disease than it really is. On referring to the diagram it will be seen that in simple prolapse, without torsion, when the uterus has assumed the position indicated by figure 3, if one attempted to introduce the sound, its point must be directly backwards, and this being the case, the mobility of the uterus at all times admitting of considerable change of position by pressure, &c., it will often be impossible to judge whether the whole organ be simply inclined backwards, or is really more or less bent upon itself, and in this way, I feel assured, that many cases of simple prolapse are considered to be cases of slight retroversion.

Symptomatology.

We come now to the consideration of the most important, and yet, alas! the most unsatisfactory part of our inquiry, viz., the symptoms by which the above lesions can be detected. All my experience has led me fully to appreciate the truth of Professor Simpson's statement made in 1843, to the following effect:—"There can be no doubt of the fact, that there seems to be no organ in which there is a less strict relation observable between the intensity and character of the existing pathological disease, and the intensity and character of the accompanying symptoms, or between the exact nature of the structural lesions that are present, and the exact combination and succession of functional derangements to which they give rise."* And again, in 1848, in the paper already referred to, he remarks :—" In uterine disease, as in pregnancy, the same specific affection of the organ excites sometimes very different phenomena in different cases; and the same specific phenomena frequently result from affections of the organ which are entirely at variance with each other in their pathological character, in their course, and in the treatment required."† In the disease under our consideration for example, I have met with the greatest possible variety in the symptoms complained of, where a physical examination revealed the greatest possible correspondence between the pathological conditions of the various cases ; I have found enlargement and ulceration of the cervix uteri in a case examined for another purpose, and where there was no detectable aberration from robust health. I have found the slightest of all the forms of disease mentioned above, *i.e.*, the first stage of cervico-metritis, (*vide* p. 27,) where the constitutional disturbance was very grave, and the symptoms had continued a long time; and lastly, I have known the symptoms to connect themselves as completely with some distant organ, as the head, the stomach, the heart, the mamma, or the extremities, that indirect causes alone led me to suspect the uterine complication; and yet in all these varieties (save the first case, which was not treated) such a marked improvement followed the cure of the uterine affection, as to leave little doubt respecting the important part it played in each. It must not be supposed, however, from the above remarks, that I wish it to be understood, that we possess no criteria in the form of symptoms by which to judge of the probable or positive presence of uterine disease in any given case, but rather that we cannot determine, from an examination of the subjective symptoms, as to the exact nature or intensity of the uterine affection. In a large majority of cases there is but

* Monthly Journal, 1843, p. 553. † Dublin Journal, May, 1848, p. 376.

little difficulty in arriving at a definite conclusion as to the existence of uterine disease, while on the other hand it is very hazardous to risk one's accuracy of diagnosis, by attempting to decide upon the exact nature and extent of the affection until the case has been submitted to a rigid local examination. It is only by means of the speculum and a digital examination, that we can obtain that precise information which is essential ere we can prognosticate the probable result of the case, or, as we shall see presently, ere we can determine the course of treatment which offers the best chance of success. When speaking of the pathology of this disease, I should have observed that it occurs with not very unequal frequency in the single or married, and in the latter, whether they have had families or not; the disease presents very nearly the same character in all the three classes of patients, and calls for pretty much the same treatment in each. As, however, any examination of the uterus in the unmarried female, and more especially when the speculum requires to be used, is far too serious an operation to be unwarrantably proposed, it is of great importance that a medical man should be fully convinced of its absolute necessity ere he ventures to have recourse to such an expedient, or even to suggest the propriety of its adoption. It is impossible to lay down any rule upon this subject which will apply to all cases, but I may safely observe in a general way, that it will be rarely found necessary to have recourse to such a proceeding when a case first presents itself for treatment. But, if the diligent employment of general means do not effect the desired relief, this very want of success will afford a good foundation on which to ground our arguments as to the necessity of a local investigation.

Professor Simpson, in his paper on retroversion, gives a very clear and concise summary of the symptoms attending that disease, which are, however, so precisely similar to those accompanying many other non-malignant diseases of the uterus, that with the exception of those produced by the direct mechanical action of the misplaced organ, the description will prove equally apposite to the more comprehensive class of diseases embraced by this paper. Dr. Simpson remarks, "In retroversion, as in other morbid conditions and diseases of the unimpregnated uterus, the accompanying sympathetic derangements or symptoms are, when they are well and highly marked, more or less perfect imitations of the secondary phenomena of pregnancy. Dyspeptic and hysterical symptoms are sometimes present with local neuralgic pains in the mammæ; in some portion of the vertebral column; or what is still more frequent, in the parietes of the abdomen or chest; and more especially in a limited spot beneath the left mamma. * * * Symptoms of weight, tension and bearing down in the regions of the uterus and rectum, with dragging at the loins, and in the regions of the uterine ligaments, are very common. Pains often stretch down one or both lower extremities, and in general all the symptoms, local and constitutional, which I have alluded to, are aggravated more or less, by exercise in the erect position; and they are more particularly liable to be increased in their intensity, when the uterus becomes periodically congested and heavier, at the recurrence of each menstrual period."*

Such is a very correct summary of the symptoms most usually met with in cases of inflammation of the uterus and its appendages; for practical purposes, however connected either with diagnosis or treatment, we must analyse the symptoms further; but before doing so I would make a remark which appears to me of great importance. When examining symptoms for diagnostic purposes we must of necessity lay the greatest stress on those which are pathognomonic, or nearly so, of the disease in question, since it follows, of necessity, that among many symptoms, the most important, in this view of the case, must be that which most accurately expresses the pathological condition with which it is connected; or in other words, the symptom which is most intimately and invariably connected with a certain pathological state is regarded as the most characteristic, independent altogether of its intrinsic severity. When, on the contrary, one is called upon to prescribe for a case, it is impossible to prevent the patient laying the greatest stress on that symptom or symptoms which are the most severe and annoying, and one is repeatedly obliged to direct the treatment specially against some

* Dublin Quarterly Journal of Medical Science, May, 1848, pp. 377–8.

symptom of peculiar distress to the patient, although fully aware that it is by no means inseparably connected with the disease in question; nay, when one knows full well that it may be entirely removed, although the disease itself remains unchanged. This distinction between the characteristic symptoms of the disease, and the symptoms constituting the chief complaint on the part of the patient, must be constantly borne in mind if one desires to avoid the endless seeming contradictions which are to be met in the reported results of various modes of treatment—for it will be found, on enquiry, that among the practitioners of the old school, (who are so accustomed to view their cases solely from a pathological starting point, that they will unhesitatingly affirm that a patient "has nothing in the world the matter with her," though racked with pain, and shattered in nerve, provided there is no pathological lesion on which they can fix their eye;) there are few who do not report as perfect cures every case which, under their treatment, is relieved of the objective symptoms of the disease under which they were labouring, or who had ceased to suffer from certain indications which they have been led to regard as pathognomonic of the disease in question. While, on the contrary, there has been too great a tendency among our homœopathic brethren to regard those patients as cured who have ceased to complain of the symptoms for which they sought relief, without employing the necessary means for ascertaining whether or not the actual pathological lesion, which originally gave rise to these phenomena, has been removed. In consequence of this, it is by no means uncommon to meet with patients who have been reported as cured of uterine inflammation, or ulceration, by some celebrated accoucheur, and, who, nevertheless, pour into your ear a long sad list of aches and pains which make life a weariness, and render them wholly unfit for their usual avocations; and, on the other hand, I have known patients report, from time to time, their supposed rapid and steady progress towards recovery, in consequence of the continued diminution of the symptoms which led them to seek advice, while the speculum revealed the unwelcome fact, that the disease itself had throughout the whole period of treatment, remained unaltered. We have thus two distinctly opposite conditions of partial cure, which are each, in their turn, reported as complete recoveries; and it comes to be an important practical question as to which species of relief is best for the patient—whether to have the pathological lesion cured, while many of the pains and discomforts continue unabated, or to have these distressing aches removed while the local affection remains unchanged.

As regards the diagnostic value of the various symptoms, perhaps the most important is the peculiar sense of weight in the hypogastrium, which is seldom, if ever, altogether absent in this disease. This symptom consists of a peculiar sense of dragging heaviness in the uterine region, most distinctly perceived in the erect posture, and accompanied at all times with an amount of general *malaise* and discomfort altogether disproportioned to the actual amount of pain—the pain itself is seldom violent, except in acute metritis, and yet be it ever so slight, it is invariably spoken of as most wearing and wearisome. In many cases, indeed, the general effects so far exceed the local discomfort, that the patient confines her complaints to the feeling of universal weariness and *malaise*, and it is only by direct interrogation that you ascertain the existence of the pain in question; and, nevertheless, as a proof that the latter is the exciting cause of the former, if you remove the hypogastric heaviness, the patient at once becomes much brighter and cheerful, and almost invariably describes her relief as "the removal of a great weight."

Next in diagnostic importance is the presence of *leucorrhœa;* this symptom, however, cannot be viewed as absolutely pathognomic of inflammation of the uterine neck, seeing that in some cases of well-marked disease, it is so small in quantity that it does not reach the vulva, and its existence is not made known, until by the aid of the speculum, you obtain a view of the *os uteri*, and then perceive the canal filled with a true leucorrhœal secretion. While, on the other hand, an occasional leucorrhœa must not at once be set down as infallibly indicating the presence of uterine inflammation, seeing that in many patients, the normal periodic congestion of the uterus at each menstrual crisis is accompanied by a discharge of this character, which, in such cases, appears either for a few days before or after each period.

With these exceptions, I believe we may unhesitatingly affirm, that, in every case of continued leucorrhœa, there exists more or less chronic inflammation of a larger or smaller portion of the uterus; and, moreover, we may also conclude, that however much a patient may improve in general health, her uterine affection cannot be considered as cured until the leucorrhœa shall have altogether ceased; nay, more, seeing that some degree of inflammation may exist without any external appreciable leucorrhœa, it follows that we cannot actually pronounce upon the complete cure of any such case without the aid of the speculum.

Menstrual irregularity, either as respects the time, quantity or quality of the secretion, should perhaps hold the next place in point of importance among the symptoms of this disease, whose presence will aid us in diagnosis. In a large majority of those suffering from uterine inflammation, there will be found some more or less marked abnormality in this respect. The menses will be either too early or too late in their appearance, the flow will be more or less unsteady during the time of its existence, and the duration will be either unusually shortened or prolonged. Again: the quantity will vary from the merest trace to an amount well meriting the title of menorrhagia; and yet, again, the quality of the secretion will show every variety, from an almost colourless watery fluid to a thick viscous material, more like tar in its aspect, and vying with ink in its blackness. As, however, all those, and many more varieties may be met with in company with one and the same organic lesion, it is obvious, that while the fact of any menstrual irregularity may lead us to suspect the existence of uterine inflammation, the peculiar abnormality will be of little service in enabling us to decide upon the exact morbid condition of the uterus itself.

Painful menstruation is another symptom of very frequent occurrence, but of little diagnostic value, save in some few cases where there is reason to suspect a mechanical cause for the impeded function.

Pains of various kinds, from a mere sense of weariness to an almost continued agony which prevents all motion, are found occurring in the loins and across the sacrum; the variety, however, and diagnostic uncertainty of these symptoms are so great that, common though they be, we cannot be guided by them in our decision as to the nature of the case. The same remarks apply to the pains in the ovarian and iliac regions, and that under the left mamma, which, though proving so intensely troublesome in practice, are of little if any value as elements of diagnosis, beyond the fact that their presence may lead us to suspect the possibility of the existence of uterine inflammation, and thus induce us to follow up our inquiries in that direction, for the purpose of obtaining some surer guide to our decision.

Let us, now, for a moment examine the symptoms which especially lead patients suffering under this malady to apply for relief.

Beyond all question, the symptom which causes the patient most distress in this disease, is the general feeling of *debility* that almost invariably accompanies it. In the vast majority of patients who apply for relief, the very first thing they complain of is this same weakness, and, on inquiry, you find it has gradually come upon them, assailing them with slow but steady steps, and gradually incapacitating them for one duty after another, until, in severe cases, the sufferer is completely prostrated, and drags on a weary life of confinement to the bed or couch, with occasional airings in a horizontal wheel-chair. Nothing can be more complete than the enervation consequent upon this disease; and what adds so vastly to the trials of the patient, and the distress of all around her, is the fact that but few minds are strong enough to bear up against this protracted debility, and, in consequence, we have, in addition to the physical symptoms, a variety of mental ones, embracing a large field of moral phenomena, from slight irritability and caprice to more or less complete mental aberration.

The next symptom as respects the frequency with which it constitutes the chief cause of the patient's application for advice, is *headache*. This might almost be surmised from the remarks I have just made, respecting the very common union of physical with moral or mental symptoms, as it is notorious that but few morbid mental conditions occur unaccompanied by some degree of pain in the head. As might be supposed, the character of headache complained of varies immensely, but one of the most frequent and, at the same time, intractable varieties, is pain, more or less pressive, on the vortex, accompanied by heat, sometimes amounting to severe burning, which appears to extend deep into the brain.

Almost equal in frequency, as a cause of complaint, is *pain in the back;* this also varies much in its specific character, being at times much more acute, while at others it resembles more a dull aching, similar to that occurring to the healthy when over-fatigued. It also is frequently accompanied by a sense of burning in the part affected, which proves peculiarly harrassing to the patient. This pain in the back, when it constitutes at all a chief source of complaint, is usually the symptom of all others from which the patient craves relief, and any amelioration in this respect at once impresses her with the conviction that she must be decidedly better, and yet, there is scarcely any symptom connected with this disease which is of less value diagnostically, since it may altogether disappear, while the uterine affection remains unimproved (though this is rare); or, again, which is much more common, the uterus may be restored to perfect health, while the pain in the back continues unabated, or even increases in severity.

Various neuralgic symptoms occupy the next step in the order of frequency, and, then, may be placed *leucorrhœa*, which thus comes to occupy a position vastly different from that which it held among the elements of diagnosis; but, the fact is, that unless the discharge is copious, the patient, seldom, if ever, lays any stress on its existence, except, indeed, where some former medical attendant has told her that her debility and other causes of complaint are traceable to that source.

Much more might be advanced respecting the symptomatology of this disease, but I feel my subject so much too extensive for a paper, that I must resist the temptation of dilating upon these points, and proceed at once to say a few words respecting

Prognosis.

The peculiar characteristic of this disease, as far as my own experience goes, is its tendency to remain unchanged; it certainly has no great tendency to become worse, and as little disposition does there appear to be to spontaneous amendment.

I have known of cases which remained for months, or even years, without any appreciable variation; and I have repeatedly been consulted by patients whose sufferings had extended over periods of ten, fifteen, or more years, and who, on examination, did not exhibit proofs of graver disease than are to be met with in persons whose ailments are distinctly referable to some recent cause. Dr. Bennet obviously holds much the same opinion, and explains it by reference to the periodic congestion of the uterus, which occurs at each menstrual crisis, and which congestion so nearly approaches to inflammation, that it is nothing extraordinary to find it giving rise to an aggravated condition of the pre-existing disease. In consequence of this tendency to periodic aggravation, the disease never gets, as it were, an opportunity of spontaneous cure, for long ere the process is half completed the recurring congestion reproduces the morbid condition, and thus tends to perpetuate the malady. Such being the character of the local disease, let us see what is the prevailing tendency of the general derangement which accompanies it. I have already stated that the amount of general derangement varies immensely, and that while many patients with the slightest form of uterine inflammation have completely shattered health, you may occasionally meet with considerable enlargement, and even ulceration of the cervix uteri, unaccompanied by any appreciable symptoms of ill-health, and, it seems to me, that, in many respects, it remains still an open question, how far in cases of general ill-health, accompanied by uterine inflammation, the local disease is to be considered the true point of departure from the healthy state. This is a question full of deep and practical interest, and while, for some reasons, I regret that time will not admit of my entering upon its consideration, still as I do not possess materials upon which I could found a conclusive opinion, I should have been obliged to confine myself to the throwing out of various hints which might have guided those who felt inclined to pursue the question. It is a question, however, of which I shall certainly not lose sight, and anything of practical interest which may result from my investigations can be made known at some future period. Three things, however, are quite certain—viz., 1st. That in the vast majority of females who are suffering from inflammation of the cervix uteri and its consequences, the general health is far from good; 2d. That such derangement of health, for the most part, proves extremely difficult to relieve, except by the employment of remedies known to have a specific action on the uterus; and 3rd. That although many females may be, to a considerable degree, restored to health without the local affection being cured, yet it but rarely happens that such persons become really or permanently well until the uterus is restored to its normal state. Founded upon these data, we may form the following prognosis in the great majority of cases—viz., that, if the case is left to nature, the probability of a spontaneous cure is exceedingly small, whereas if submitted to treatment for the purpose of restoring the general derangement, such treatment will not prove entirely successful, unless combined with means which will, at the same time, cure the uterine disease. The reason for this guarded mode of expression will be seen immediately. As regards the time necessary to effect a cure, it, of course, varies much, but it is always considerable, and a physician will do well to be very guarded in his promises in respect to the time when his patient may calculate on a complete cure. This slow progress is not to be wondered at when we consider that every month there is a considerable risk of a relapse, and, accordingly, it is only from month to month that we can be assured of having gained any step towards recovery. Beyond the question of time, however, the prognosis may be decidedly favourable, as the vast majority of patients recover if judiciously treated. Let us now, therefore, proceed to the examination of the most practical and important part of the whole subject—viz., the

Therapeutics of this Disease.

The following observations are founded chiefly on the results of my own experience in the treatment of 180 cases, an abstract of which will be found in the Appendix that accompanies this paper. Three months ago Drs. Black and Ker forwarded to the majority of my colleagues a schedule of questions, which I had drawn up for the purpose of eliciting information upon this subject, which might advantageously have been embodied with the following remarks. Up to the present moment, however, (Sep. 6th) I have only received one of these schedules, and as I find that the analysis of my own cases will occupy all the remaining time which can be allotted to this paper, I have limited my remarks to the latter, and shall let the schedule, or schedules, should more arrive, speak for themselves.

Before proceeding to analyse the cases which are to be found in the Appendix, I must say a few words regarding their selection, and the rules by which I have been guided in making the accompanying abstract. As regards the cases themselves, they have been selected from among all those which I have attended during my residence at Brighton, a period of $5\frac{1}{2}$ years, and they constitute the majority of the cases of uterine disease which have come under my notice during that period. I have, however, omitted almost all cases of tumours and malignant diseases of the uterus and its appendages, and have taken no notice of many which I lost sight of so early in the treatment that no opinion could be formed of the result of the remedies prescribed. It will be further observed, that only 70 of the whole number, or little more than one-third, were subjected to examination, and hence it follows, that I cannot speak with *absolute* certainty as to the existence of inflammation of the uterus, or its consequences in every case; nevertheless, I have carefully applied the principles laid down in the remarks I made upon diagnosis, for the purpose of avoiding error as far as possible, and by comparing the characters of the unexamined cases with those which were submitted to this method of diagnosis, and proved to be suffering from the disease in question, I feel confident that at least the vast majority were actually suffering from the same local affection. For it will be remembered that when treating of the diagnosis, I remarked, that while it was impossible to decide, from the subjective symptoms, as to the exact nature, and still less, as to the degree of severity, of the uterine disease; yet it was by no means difficult to determine, with a large measure of accuracy, as to the existence or non-existence of some phase of uterine inflammation; and on the other hand it may be observed, that in the whole of the cases examined, distinct evidence of inflammation was detected, thus proving that the means of diagnosing the probable existence of the disease are very trustworthy. It would serve no useful purpose to explain the various reasons why the whole cases were not examined, since so many different causes operated in the different cases; but with the exception of a few of the slighter ones, and of those which I treated early in my homœopathic career,—at a time when trusting to what I had read in homœopathic works, I had fancied that such cases would easily yield to general treatment alone,—I can safely affirm, that it was not because I concluded there was no detectable uterine disease that I abstained from this only absolute method of verifying my diagnosis. As regards the rules by which I have been guided in drawing up the abstract, I have only a few remarks to offer. As respects the chief symptoms, I have invariably noted only those for which the patient specially sought relief; or which, during the course of the treatment, constituted the chief source of her complaint. My reason for doing so must be obvious, because, in the first place, had I confined myself to the more purely diagnostic symptoms, I should have failed altogether in individualizing the cases; and secondly, as the patient's impression respecting improvement or otherwise will, for the most part, depend upon the amelioration or the contrary of these chief causes of her complaint, it follows that no true comparison could be made between the characteristic symptoms and the effects of the remedies employed, had any other course been adopted. It is, however, of importance to bear this fact in mind, since the absence of any symptom in the abstract is no proof that it did not occur in the patient; one or two examples will make this clear. Of the 180 patients referred to, 134 had, more or less, distinctly marked leucorrhœa, whereas this sympton is only reported twenty-nine times as being a chief cause of complaint. Again, only eleven cases are reported as suffering from amenorrhœa, whereas in thirty-six the menses were absent. On the contrary in the column devoted to the state of the menstrual functions, I have endeavoured to indicate its precise condition in every instance in as far as that could be done without entering into details, and hence a summary of these conditions, such as is given in table 5, affords precise numerical information respecting the comparative frequency of each symptom. Again: regarding the notice of the medicines, I have strictly limited my remarks to those which proved more or less decidedly beneficial. At first I attempted to make a perfect transcript of the treatment, but I soon found that such a course was both useless and unintelligible without the notes appended to each prescription, as in those who were any length of time under treatment, there were almost invariably one or more intercurrent attacks requiring specific remedies, and which would have appeared altogether inexplicable if appended to the short summary of chief symptoms, which alone find a place in the abstract. I have invariably noted the potency in which the medicine was given, and the usual mode of administering the medicine was as follows:—in a few cases I allowed an interval of six or eight days to elapse after each course of medicine, and occasionally I gave single doses every third or fourth day; but in most of the cases the plan pursued was, to give medicines daily for six days and then wait one day, if the patients were seen every week; or if only seen once a fortnight, as was sometimes the case with convalescents, they took three short courses lasting three days each, with an interval of two days between each course. The order in which the medicines are put down is the order in which they were administered; I have not, however, indicated whether the remedies were given in immediate succession, or whether other medicines had been administered unsuccessfully during the interval. Lastly, as regards the objective uterine symptoms and their local treatment, whenever such was had recourse to, I have noted them separately, and in such a manner as to avoid the possibility of confusion. These preliminary remarks will serve to introduce the Appendix to your notice, and I shall now proceed to detail the results to which my experience has brought me, and also to indicate the many points which still demand patient investigation, ere we can pronounce any decided opinion regarding them.

According to the usual method of selecting a homœopathic remedy, we must choose one whose pathogenetic effects bear a close, if not exact, resemblance to the symptoms of the disease we are about to treat. If therefore the disease in question be characterized by two series of phenomena, composed respectively of subjective sensations and objective symptoms, we must select for its cure a remedy capable not only of producing the peculiar sensations complained of by the patient, but of doing so in conjunction with the objective phenomena which equally constitute the disease; and if we fail in this, we at the same time fail in selecting a truly homœopathic remedy. Let us therefore turn to the *Materia Medica*, and ascertain whether it is rich in remedies which have been proved capable of producing the various symptoms complained of by females suffering under *uterine inflammation*, and at the same time of inducing those local changes in the uterine tissues which especially characterise this complaint. On going over the whole of the remedies which have been proved by Hahnemann and his followers, with the exception of those introduced by Dr. Mure and others within the last few years, I can only find four purely pathogenetic symptoms which indicate organic changes in the uterus, and these are as follow:—

1. "*Irregularity of the os uteri*," as a symptom of *natrum carbonicum*, reported by Noack and Trinks, but not to be found in Hahnemann's Chronischen Krankheiten, which contains the original proving.

2. "*Metritis*," as a sympton of *secale cornutum*, reported in the proving of this remedy, which appeared in the Appendix to the British Journal of Homœopathy, and where it is quoted on the authority of Spajrani and L'Admirault.

3. "*Softness of uterus*," a most indefinite and not very intelligible term, as a symptom of *opium*, reported by Noack and Trinks, but not to be found in Hahnemann's Reine Arzneimittellehre, where the medicine was first proved.

4. And lastly, "*Swelling of the cervix*," as a symptom of *cantharis*, reported by Noack and Trinks, in connection with burning in the neck of the bladder, and other symptoms of inflammation of that organ.

With the exception of these I cannot find any objective symptom connected with the uterus, which has not been obtained *ex usu in morbis*, a source far too subject to fallacy to warrant our trusting to it exclusively in our selection of remedies. This extreme paucity of objective uterine symptoms cannot be wondered at, when we consider the obstacles in the way of obtaining such evidence in our ordinary methods of proving; for not to mention the difficulty of obtaining female provers, and the immensely greater difficulty of inducing such to submit during the taking of the remedy, to repeated examinations by the speculum, obstacles of themselves sufficient to deter most men from entering upon such an investigation; it is very seldom warrantable to continue the experimental taking of medicine until such time as actual organic changes have been produced by its toxic influence. Being thus, in a great measure, shut out from this, the only absolutely trustworthy method of proving our remedies, is there any other way by which we can judge, with some measure of accuracy, respecting the action of any medicine on the uterus, and from which we can infer, with tolerable certainty, that organic changes have either actually taken place, or would do so, if the experiment were continued? The only other method of investigation that I am aware of is, that of observing carefully the effects of various medicines upon the uterine functions; and this seems to have been most extensively done, since there are but few medicines in whose provings, various functional derangements of the uterus, as for instance, respecting the periodicity and character of the menses, have not been observed. Unfortunately, for our purpose however, it has been most distinctly proved, that there is no constant correspondence between the condition of the uterus and the state and mode of performance of its functions; and surely a remedy capable of producing a given derangement of function, accompanied by a certain morbid condition of the uterus, cannot be viewed as truly homœopathic to the same functional derangement in association with an altogether different local state —so that we cannot arrive at any degree of certainty in this way.

One other method remains open to us—viz., by investigating the morbid secretions produced by a medicine, and comparing that with the secretion accompanying the disease, and if this were capable of being fully carried out, and an exact correspondence detected, I should imagine the consequent selection of the remedy to be decidedly trustworthy. In connection with this subject I have examined all the leucorrhœal symptoms in the *Materia Medica*, and when analysed they give the following results:—*Leucorrhœa* is reported as a symptom of between 70 and 80 medicines; in 11 it is characterised as *copious*, and in 12 the duration is mentioned. In 8 the mere fact of leucorrhœa occurring is reported, without detailing its character or concomitants; and in 10 the symptoms appear to have been chiefly derived "*ex usu in morbis.*" Now, the duration of the discharge is one of the most important characteristics, in as far as occasional or temporary leucorrhœa can never be viewed as pathognomonic of an inflammatory condition of the uterus; experience having taught us that very slight and transient causes (mere mental excitement in some cases), are often capable of producing a more or less copious, though temporary vaginal discharge. On referring again to the *Materia Medica*, regarding the length of time during which the leucorrhœa lasted in the different provings, we find, as I before remarked, only 12 instances in which this is noted, and of these, with one exception, 10 days is the longest period observed. The exceptional case is that of *ignatia*, concerning which Hahnemann reports, as a symptom, "long-continued leucorrhœa."

These facts collectively lead us to the conclusion, that as yet we have no absolutely certain guide in our *Materia Medica* towards the selection of the most suitable remedies for this disease, and as corollaries to the above we may conclude—first, that should homœopathic treatment fail in any degree in relieving this disease, such want of success is no proof of any defect in our law of healing; and, secondly, if other than ordinary homœopathic treatment is at present required to effect a complete cure in certain cases of this disease, we must not infer from this that the time will not some day arrive when purely specific treatment may be found capable of effecting all that can be desired.

In the tables, which occur in the Appendix, it will be found that I have classed together those who were "cured" and those who were "greatly benefitted," and I had many reasons for doing so. 1. In dispensary practice it is almost impossible to ascertain the exact number of cures, as so many of the patients fail in reporting themselves. 2. Very many patients will say that they feel quite well, and will return to their ordinary avocations, while continuing at times to experience unpleasant sensations, which would induce a more fastidious person to remain under treatment. Under the head, therefore, of "cured or greatly benefitted," I have classed together those patients who reported themselves as cured, and those who voluntarily gave up treatment, and whose reports for some time previous had shown steady and great improvement. I have, however, invariably distinguished those who, though greatly benefitted, had not felt so for a sufficiently long time to warrant the conclusion that they would continue to enjoy comparative health, and have denoted these as having "left treatment too early to judge."

It may, perhaps, be asserted that I have placed the standard of cure too high, and I quite believe that all the cases reported by me in the combined form of "cured or greatly benefitted," would have appeared in most statistical accounts under the simple title of "cured." But I have purposely exercised this precaution, lest I should fall into the error which I referred to in an early part of this paper (p. 38), and which leads to such misapprehension when comparing the results of different kinds of treatment. As in the abstract of the cases I have reported the exact condition, as far as known to me, of every patient at the close of the treatment, the blending of the two degrees of benefit cannot mislead any one.

On referring to the first table in the Appendix, which gives the general results of the cases treated, we find, that of 180 cases reported, 112 were cured or greatly benefitted, 51 received benefit, and 17 remained unchanged: this gives a per centage of 62¼ cured or greatly benefitted, and only about 9½ per cent. of cases unchanged, an amount of success which, I believe, will be considered very fair by any one who has had much experience in the treatment of this disease. In the general table, however, there are included 22 cases which are still under treatment, and 34 who left treatment, or were lost sight of, too early to judge accurately of the result; these, therefore, must be deducted before an accurate estimate of the success of the treatment can be obtained. Of the 22 cases still under treatment, 10 are reported as greatly benefitted, and 12 as somewhat benefitted; and of the 34 who left treatment too early to judge, 19 are reported as cured or greatly benefitted, 11 as having received some benefit, and 4 as unchanged. Making the necessary deductions, therefore, from the gross number, the tables would stand thus—Cases whose results are fully known 124, of whom 83 were cured or greatly benefitted, 28 were somewhat relieved, and 13 continued unchanged; thus making the correct per centage of cure $66\frac{9}{10}$.

I have already stated (p. 46), that early in my homœopathic career I had been led to expect such perfectly satisfactory results from general treatment alone, that for a considerable time I trusted entirely to constitutional remedies; so many cases, however, occurred to me where my best endeavours proved unsuccessful, that after two or three years' experience of the constitutional treatment, I resolved on trying the effect of combining local treatment with it, for the purpose if possible of doing more good to my patients. The reasons which led me to adopt this course are too numerous and would require too much detail to explain; suffice it to say, that it was founded on the general reports of the degree of success of other homœopathic practitioners in this disease, as well as my own; and, moreover, I did not make the change until I had examined the whole subject well, and had been led to conclude that the local treatment, so far as it was medicinal, was, in point of fact, as truly homœopathic to the disease in question as the general treatment itself, nay, in some respects more so, since, as I have already shown, we do not possess pathogenetic symptoms corresponding accurately to the disease under our notice. The local means which I have had recourse to have been—1. the water douche, employed either warm or cold, and, in some few cases, using sea-water in place of the pure element; 2. various mechanical means introduced to the profession by Dr. Simpson; and, 3. various caustics, especially the *nitrate of silver*.

Of the *douche* I need say but little: you all know its value, and there would be no hesitation on the part of any of you to prescribe it. I have found it, in many cases, a very useful adjuvant, but only one case of ulceration is reported (*i. e.* 23rd), wherein it, alone, proved sufficient to cure the disease.

As respects the mechanical treatment, I must confess my results do not at all come up to the expectations I was led to form of it, from the statements of Dr. Simpson, Dr. Protheroe Smith, and others, who have had recourse to it extensively. One case (84) was evidently much benefitted by the repeated introduction of the uterine sound into the retroverted uterus and the replacement of the organ by its means. This little operation I performed twice a week for two or three months, leaving the sound in the uterine cavity for some hours, during which treatment the patient greatly improved in general health, the uterus lost, to a considerable extent, its tendency to retrovert, and the patient married, soon became pregnant, bore a healthy child, after which the uterus did not assume its abnormal position. In one case of considerable engorgement of the uterus, with slight prolapse, but no other mal-position (case 103), I employed Scofield's porcelain pessary, which has the advantage of being easily removable by the patient for the purposes of cleanliness, and after wearing it a few months the uterine symptoms completely ceased.

Of Dr. Simpson's celebrated uterine support or pessary, (I mean the one composed of a stem, to be introduced into the cavity of the uterus, a shield upon which the cervix rests, and a curved wire which serves to retain the instrument *in situ*,) I have made 9 trials with the following results :—In two it decidedly did harm, the patients being in every respect worse after its employment than before; in one the benefit was but slight, and in six the patients recovered, but in three of these the treatment was immensely aided by the use of Caustics, thus leaving $\frac{1}{3}$ only of the cases as decidedly benefitted by this means alone; the cases referred to are Nos. 19, 29, and 73. Still further, however, to diminish the real success of this mode of treatment, it must be mentioned that, in case 73, the instrument caused so much local discomfort, after the patient had worn it $3\frac{1}{2}$ months, that I was obliged to remove it, and I then found that the uterus, though benefitted, had by no means entirely lost its tendency to retrovert. The rationale of this means of treatment has, I think, been much misunderstood, and hence it has been inveighed against as altogether unphilosophical. My belief is, that it acts by converting a partial into a general affection. I have already stated my belief that flexures of the uterus are the result of partial congestion of its walls; now, the introduction and retention within its cavity of a foreign body, such as the stem of Simpson's pessary, invariably increases this congestion, and causes it to spread over the whole uterus, for I have invariably found this to be the condition of the organ when the pessary has been removed. When, however, the congestion of the uterus is uniform, there no longer exists any tendency to assume a bent position, and if, after the removal of the instrument, judicious means are employed to cure the congestion, the patient is completely restored to health. I therefore look upon this mode of treatment as very similar to that of the surgeon who would intentionally break a limb which had been ill-set and healed distortedly, for the purpose of repairing the former malposition. It is, to my mind, an obvious instance of doing evil that good may come, of aggravating the existing disease because the greater is in this case the more amenable to treatment; and, although I believe but few cases really call for this method of treatment, yet in an aggravated case of retro- or anteversion, where the misplaced uterus gave rise mechanically to many symptoms, I would not hesitate to have recourse to it, provided other means had failed of giving relief.

With respect to the application of Caustics, I fear many of you will look upon the deed as very heretical, but I trust a little consideration will prove to you that it is a mode of treatment much more homœopathic in its action than may, at first sight, be supposed. When a Caustic is applied to any surface, two actions are produced, viz.—

1st. The local or chemical effect.

2nd. The general effects of its absorption when the latter takes place at all.

Now as regards *nitrate of silver*, which has been the chief local remedy employed by me, the admirable proving published in the *Austrian Journal* has shown it to act specifically on the uterus, giving rise to capillary congestion, and in some instances to hæmorrhage; and as regards its local action, it produces a diseased condition which most strikingly resembles the different stages of cervico-metritis. If, for example, in a patient suffering from the first stage of this disease, the solid Nitrate of Silver be passed up the cervical canal and retained there a few seconds, it will be found a few days after that the disease is simply aggravated, indeed it is impossible to distinguish between the first effects of the Caustic and an increase of the local mischief from any other cause. But this is not all: if the Nitrate of Silver be used freely in an irritable constitution, it will, at times, give rise to sudden enlargement and induration of the cervix, which so exactly resembles the fourth stage of cervico-metritis that nothing but the history of the case could enable one to distinguish between them. An example of this occurred in case 180. Again: the experiments of Professor Simpson, of applying pulverized Nitrate of Silver to the interior of the uterus itself, have shown that while acting locally on the uterus, it sympathetically affects the ovary, in so much as in a case of amenorrhœa, where he employed this means to endeavour to restore the menses, and where the patient died two days afterwards from other causes, he found that a graafian vesicle had been developed and ruptured, in a manner precisely analogous to what occurs at a normal menstrual period. These facts seem to me fully to warrant the conclusion that Nitrate of Silver, in *addition to its obvious chemical effects*, acts in such a manner upon the uterus when applied locally, that it may be viewed in the light of a strictly homœopathic remedy. Analagous arguments might be brought forward in respect to the only other escharotics which I have employed, viz., *pernitrate of mercury* and *potassa fusa*, both of which drugs have also a specific action on the uterus and its appendages. I may mention, that for some time past, I have combined the local with the internal use of the remedy, giving *argentum nitricum* when employing the Nitrate of Silver locally, and administering one or other of the preparations of *mercurius* when using the *pernitrate of mercury*. Lastly, I have of late been trying the effects of certain other remedies, as *kali bichromicum*, and the *clorides of gold, platinum* and *tin*, as local remedies, having been led to their employment by their homœopathicity to various phases of this disease; my results, however, are not as yet sufficiently definite to admit of my drawing any conclusions from them. On referring to table 6 it will be found, that the results of the cases treated locally as compared with those who had internal remedies only, were as follow: after making the deductions already alluded to of the cases still under treatment, and those which left too early to judge of the result, it will be found that of 41 cases examined and treated locally, 30 were cured or greatly benefitted; while of 105 cases treated entirely by general remedies, only 63 recovered; or, in other words, while $73\frac{1}{6}$ per cent. of those treated locally were cured or greatly benefitted, only 60 per cent. of those who were treated by general remedies obtained the same amount of relief. If, however, we examine a little closer, we shall find a still greater balance in favor of the employment of local treatment, for it must be remembered that in almost every instance I commenced with general treatment only, and did not think of having recourse to local measures until these had proved inefficient, so that it follows, that in the first place the cases not examined or treated locally embrace all the slight cases, while the 47 cases treated locally must comprehend most of the severer cases which came under my notice, excepting only the few who refused to submit to examination. And again, on examining the notes of these 47 cases I find that no less than 25 had experienced no appreciable benefit ere the local treatment was commenced, although the general remedies were sometimes persevered in for several months before a change of treatment was had recourse to. For the purpose, therefore, of comparing accurately, the results of the general and the combined general and local treatment, we must add to the 105 cases above mentioned 36 who had been previously subjected to general treatment, and of whom, at the time the local treatment was commenced, 25 had received no benefit, while 11 had experienced some degree of relief. Calculating the per centage upon these data it will be found that, while the combined local and general treatment cured or greatly benefitted $73\frac{1}{6}$ per cent., only $44\frac{1}{3}$

per cent. obtained the same benefit from purely constitutional treatment, and this in spite of the fact already mentioned, that the class treated locally consisted, of necessity, of a much graver set of cases than those where general treatment alone was had recourse to. As examples of local treatment proving successful where general remedies had been found more or less insufficient, I would refer to cases 27, 46, 81, 84, 127, and 174. The usual arguments against the employment of local remedies are, that while they cure the local manifestation of the disease, they leave the constitutional derangement unchanged. But this argument cannot apply to the treatment I am advocating, wherein the constitutional is invariably combined with the local treatment, and thus both phases of the disease are attacked. Much more could be said upon this subject, and a careful perusal of the abstract of the 180 cases treated, will show that it contains materials wherewith most, if not all, of the usual arguments against this mode of treatment might be refuted, but I cannot dilate upon them now.

In the abstract will be found a large number of tables, from which materials could be drawn capable of furnishing much interesting and important information, some points of which I will now endeavour to lay before you.

1. *Influence of Age.* In this respect it will be found that the greatest number of cases occurred between 20 and 25; next in order comes those between 15 and 20; then between 30 and 35; next, between 25 and 30; then, 35 and 40; and lastly, from 40 upwards. If we confine our observations to the cases subjected to examination, or in other words, to with few exceptions the graver forms of the disease, we shall find that the greatest number of cases occurred between 30 and 35; next in order came the periods of 25 to 30, and 35 to 40, which present an equal number of cases; then follows the period of 20 to 25; then 15 to 20; and lastly, that of from 40 upwards.

As regards the curability of the disease at the different ages, it will be found, after making the usual deductions, that of the whole number treated, those between 30 and 35 proved the most manageable, no less than 82½ per cent. having been cured or greatly benefitted. Then follow the cases occurring between 20 and 25, of which 76⅓ per cent. yielded to treatment; between 35 and 40, 61 per cent. were cured or greatly benefitted; between 40 and upwards, 58⅓ per cent. were cured; between 15 and 20, the per centage was 56½; and lastly, from 25 to 30, half yielded to the means employed. Again: confining our observations to the graver cases, we find that between 35 and 40, no less than 84½ per cent. yielded to treatment; of those aged 40 and upwards, 75 per cent. were cured or greatly benefitted; between 20 and 25, 66⅔ per cent. were cured or greatly benefitted; while between 30 and 35, only 46¼ per cent. yielded to treatment. Thus, we find, as a general result, that on the whole the greatest number of cases occur between the ages of 30 and 40, and that it is at that time also most amenable to treatment, with this peculiarity, that while among the slighter cases the most unmanageable ones occur between 35 and 40, among the graver ones the period from 30 to 35 comprehends the cases most difficult to treat.

2. *Influence of Social Condition.* A reference to table 13 shows us that of the 70 cases examined, 46 were married, and 24 were single, showing a considerable preponderance, as might be expected, in favour of marriage, as an exciting cause of this disease. As regards the treatment however, the married appear to be more readily cured, since 30 out of the 46 were cured or greatly benefitted, *i. e.* 65½ per cent.; whereas only 50 per cent. of the unmarried received the same amount of benefit; thus showing that the disease though of less frequent occurrence, is of a more inveterate character in the unmarried female.

3. *Influence of the state of the Uterine Functions.* From table 5 it appears, that in 52 cases the menses were regular, and of these $72\frac{9}{10}$ per cent. were cured or greatly benefitted. The commonest abnormality appears to have been an increase of the menstrual discharge, 43 cases having shown that symptom, and of these 53½ per cent. yielded to treatment. Next in frequency, we meet with the complete absence of this secretion, 36 cases of amenorrhœa being reported, of which $70\frac{9}{10}$ per cent. were cured. Scanty mentsruation occurs almost as frequently, there having been 35 cases, of whom $54\frac{1}{6}$ per cent. yielded to the treatment employed. Dysmenorrhœa is reported as having occurred 25 times, of whom 50 per cent. were cured or greatly

benefitted. On the whole it appears that whereas irregularity as respects quantity is much the most frequent of the uterine abnormalities, it is by no means the most intractable; while irregularities as regards time, though less frequent, are much more difficult to manage, for it appears that of 22 cases where the period was accelerated, only 23 per cent. yielded to treatment, while of 9 cases wherein it was delayed, 33⅓ per cent. were cured or greatly benefitted.

4. *Influence of the Duration of the Disease on its Curability.* The 3rd table in the Appendix shows us that a large majority of the accompanying cases was of long standing, no less than 61 having been upwards of one year ill, while 32 of these had suffered many years; indeed of the whole 180 cases, 19 only could be considered as of recent origin. The influence of the duration of the illness on the curability of the disease is as might be expected, progressive, since of 43 who were less than twelve months ill, 74½ per cent. recovered. Of 29 whose length of illness varied from one to six years, 62 per cent. were cured or greatly benefitted; while beyond that time the per centage of recovery fell to 50.

5. *Average length of Treatment.* If we strike the average of all the cases cured or greatly benefitted, as given in table 4, we shall find that it gives rather more than 5¾ months for the period during which the treatment was continued; and if we subdivide the table into sections, we find that of the whole 83 cases cured, 50 or 60¼ per cent. recovered within six months; while 23, or 27¾ per cent. required various periods, from six months to upwards of two years, to effect a cure. And of 7 the duration of the treatment cannot be accurately calculated as they were only seen occasionally, and often at considerable intervals.

6. *Influence of the Presence of Leucorrhœa on the Curability of the Disease.* I have already mentioned, that of the 180 cases reported, 134 had more or less well marked leucorrhœa, and as this symptom is one of great diagnostic value, it will be interesting to examine somewhat carefully its influence upon the duration and curability of the disease; for this purpose I have prepared a complete set of tables, being Nos. 15 to 19 of the series. The first point we may notice here is the general

result, viz., that of the 83 cures whose results can be sufficiently traced, 66, or $79\frac{1}{2}$ per cent. were suffering from leucorrhœa. Of the 28 somewhat benefitted, 10, or $35\frac{1}{3}$ per cent. showed this symptom; while the whole of the 13 who remained unchanged, presented this symptom. Separating the examined from the unexamined cases, we find that 73 per cent. of the cases who recovered under the use of general treatment alone, had, more or less, leucorrhœa, in 44 per cent. of whom it was recorded as copious; while of the 30 cases cured by combined general and local treatment, $66\frac{2}{3}$ per cent. had leucorrhœa, and $33\frac{1}{3}$ per cent. are reported as having had it copiously.

As respects the Age. Leucorrhœa occurred on the whole most frequently between 30 and 35, while the greatest number of copious cases were between 30 and 40, especially during the latter half of that period. With respect to curability, the cases characterized by this symptom whose ages were between 20 and 25, were found to yield most readily to treatment, and also the greatest proportionate number of cases with copious leucorrhœa were cured during the same period; while on the contrary, the most intractable cases accompanied by this symptom, ranged between 25 and 35. Of the 66 patients who exhibited this symptom and recovered, 36 were married and 30 were single, so that the difference between the two classes is not marked. If, however, we examine the social condition of the whole 134 cases who were suffering from leucorrhœa, we find that 65 of these were married, while 39 only were single, showing a large preponderating frequency of the occurrence of this symptom among married females. In connection with the state of the uterine functions, leucorrhœa has more frequently accompanied regular menstruation than any of its abnormalities, and among the latter, it has been most frequently associated with copious menstruation; next in order, comes scanty menses; then amenorrhœa; then dysmenorrhœa, and what would hardly have been expected, it occurs least frequently when the menses themselves were prolonged. As might have been anticipated, the comparative frequency of the occurrence of this symptom increases as the cases are more and more chronic, so that while $84\frac{1}{2}$ per cent. of the cases which have been many years ill are characterized by this system, and 83 per cent. of those which have suffered from two to six years, are afflicted in like manner, only 58 per cent., or little more than one half of those who have more recently lost their health, are found to suffer from this common cause of female delicacy. Lastly, respecting the length of time required to complete a cure, we find, by referring to table 19, that the average length of time during which the treatment lasted, was $6\frac{1}{2}$ months, being about three weeks above the average of the whole cases, irrespective of the existence of this symptom.

7. *Influences of the various concomitant Symptoms in the Curability of this Disease.*—Table No. 11 furnishes us with an account of the frequency with which the various concomitant symptoms presented themselves as chief causes of complaint, and also informs us of the results of treatment in every case. Of these, as I have previously remarked, by far the most frequent is *debility*, it having been reported nearly twice as often as any other. As regards the curability of cases characterized by this symptom, we find that of 95 cases wherein debility constituted a chief cause of complaint, 54, or about 58 per cent. yielded to treatment. Next in frequency we find *headache*, and of 51 cases, characterized by this symptom, 28, or about 55 per cent., were cured or greatly benefitted. Of 50 cases, whose chief complaint was of *pain in the back*, 28, or about 56 per cent., were restored to health. Of 31 cases, where the sufferings were mostly of the kind included in the general term of *nervous symptoms*, 16, or about 51 per cent., were cured or greatly benefitted; and among 29 cases, where *leucorrhœa* constituted a chief source of annoyance, 19 recoveries occur, thus giving a per centage of 69. *Dyspepsia* appears the next in frequency, having been reported 27 times as characterizing the case, but the cases wherein it existed as a prominent symptom must have been somewhat mild, since no less than 22, or nearly 82 per cent., are stated to have recovered. Of the 24 patients, who especially complained of *bearing down pain*, 14, or 58 per cent., were cured or greatly benefitted; and of 18, who suffered much from characteristic *pain in the left side*, 13, or 72 per cent., were restored to health. *Menorrhagia* was the chief cause of 15 cases applying for advice, and of these 10, or

66 per cent., were cured or greatly benefitted; while of 14 cases suffering especially from *dysmenorrhœa*, only 6, or 42 per cent., are found among the list of cures. A general survey of this table will corroborate fully the remark I made previously, to the effect that many pains of frequent occurrence are by no means as frequently complained of by the patient. *Pain in the left ovary*, for example which is so generally found to exist, on questioning the patient was only referred to as a chief source of annoyance in 5 cases.

8. *Influence of the various objective Uterine Symptoms on the Curability of this Disease.* Table No. 7 affords us at a glance a comparative statement of the frequency with which the various objective uterine symptoms were observed in the 70 cases submitted to examination, and also informs us of the results of the treatment in each case. Setting aside the results of digital examination alone, we find that 36 cases were suffering from one or other of the four stages of *cervico-metritis*, of which the third stage, that of *ulceration of the cervix*, was the most frequent. In 18 cases the uterus was engorged, and in 11 there were distinct flexures. As regards the relative curability of the various conditions, we find that 77 per cent. of those suffering from inflammation and ulceration of the uterine neck were cured, while only 55 per cent. of those suffering under engorgement were restored to health. Of the 11 cases, where the uterus was more or less bent, 9 recovered. And, lastly, of 20 cases where digital examination afforded evidence of the existence of this disease, but where the speculum was not employed, neither was any local treatment had recourse to, 8 cases only, or 40 per cent., regained their health.

9. *Influence of various Remedies upon the Constitutional Symptoms, which accompany this Disease.*—In a chart which constituted Table No. 8, I had noted every remedy, and every potency of each, from which benefit accrued to the various cases, and I had noted the several characteristic symptoms which occurred in each case. It was found impossible however to reduce this to a size capable of being printed in the Journal. I have therefore simply given the names and potencies of the remedies which relieved, and have prepared Table 9, which is an analysis, as it were, of the former, limit-

ing however the observations to the 18 symptoms of most frequent occurrence, and noting only the remedies which have most frequently proved useful. It would be an almost endless business to direct your attention to all the points of interest contained in these tables, but one or two are well worthy of note; and, first, I would mention what to myself was most unexpected, viz., the remarkably high place held by *pulsatilla*, as a curative agent, in this disease. Of the 18 symptoms whose treatment I have carefully analysed, *pulsatilla* occurs as a chief remedy in no less than 16, and is superior to all in 12. Whereas, *sepia*, which stands next on the list, occurs as a chief remedy in 9 symptoms only, and as the chief in two alone. *Nux vomica* is on a par with *sepia*, in the frequency of its usefulness, and then follows *sulphur*. I must, however, guard you here against a possible error, in the use of this table, which will be best illustrated by an example—*e. g.*, of the 51 cases characterised by *headache*, Pulsatilla benefitted 35; this, however, does not prove that Pulsatilla relieved the headache in 35 cases, but that 35 cases, *relieved in their totality by Pulsatilla*, presented headache as a chief symptom, and so with all the other symptoms referred to in the table. A very strong argument in favour of the truth of homœopathy may surely be drawn from the frequency with which each case, characterised by any given symptom, yielded to one remedy, as, for instance, 35 out of 51, characterised by headache, being relieved by *pulsatilla;* 29 out of 50 cases, with *pain in the back*, being benefitted by Sepia; 10 out of 18 cases with *pain in the left side*, being relieved by *pulsatilla;* and 11 out of 15 cases with *menorrhagia*, receiving benefit from *platina*, it being impossible to conceive that anything short of a casual connection could produce such frequent recurrences of the same phenomenon. And I may perhaps be allowed to add, that while thus affording evidence of the truth of the homœopathic law, it, at the same time, indicates that my efforts to select the proper remedy for each case have not been unsuccessful; and, hence, that where a necessity for the employment of auxiliary means was felt, it was not in consequence of any want of care in conducting the homœopathic treatment. Lastly, we have some interesting facts respecting the comparative effects of high and low potencies: for it appears from table 11, that of 108 cases treated exclusively by high or low potencies, 85 were benefitted by the low, and only 23 by the high attenuations; and among the cases where both high and low potencies were used, there were 19 in which the low potencies proved decidedly the most beneficial. These results are all the more trustworthy since, throughout the treatment of the cases, I had no thought of comparing the results, and hence could not be misled by any foregone conclusion.

I must now draw this lengthy paper to a close, and I think this can best be effected by recapitulating a few of the most important conclusions which I have been led to form in connection with this disease; and these are as follow:—

1. That inflammation and ulceration of the cervix uteri is a very common cause of female delicacy.

2. That, almost without exception, cases of permanent *leucorrhœa* owe their origin to this disease, save when dependent upon much graver causes.

3. That many cases of functionally deranged menstruation, are connected with this disease.

4. That the constitutional disturbance which accompanies this disease varies so much in different cases, that no unvarying connection can be traced between the exact state of the uterus and the subjective sensations experienced by the patient.

5. That the constitutional disturbance may be greatly benefitted, if not altogether removed, by general treatment, while the state of the uterus remains unchanged, but that such cases seldom retain their health for any length of time.

6. That the local disease may be cured by purely local treatment, without any immediate relief to the constitutional disturbance. But once the local mischief is remedied, the constitutional treatment becomes more facile, and affords a much better prospect of complete success.

7. That the treatment by general remedies alone proves sufficiently successful, in slight cases, to warrant a trial of these means in almost all cases in the first instance, and warrants the hope that the time may come when local treatment may be dispensed with.

8. That of the various objective symptoms met with in this disease, the one most amenable to general treatment alone is enlargement and induration of the cervix. Case 33 illustrates this point.

9. That we have no positive evidence of a sufficient number of cures of severe cases, especially of ulceration, by general treatment alone, to warrant our persevering in the use of general remedies to the exclusion of all local treatment, in such cases as present well marked signs of uterine ulceration, and which are not benefitted locally after a fair trial of internal remedies.

10. That the local treatment of ulcerations and congestions of the uterus by *nitrate of silver*, *pernitrate of mercury* and *potassa fusa* is in strict conformity to the law of "*similia simibus curantur.*"

11. That owing to the want of correspondence between the local and general symptoms of this disease, it is not safe to pronounce positively on the local condition of any given case until it has been subjected to a careful examination by the finger and speculum.

12. That owing to this same want of correspondence, and to the extreme poverty of our *Materia Medica* in objective uterine symptoms, our treatment of this disease by general remedies must be somewhat empirical, and, for the same reason, we are not in a position to decide how far purely constitutional treatment may ultimately succeed in curing this disease.

Postscript.

I cannot allow this paper to go to press without endeavoring to guard my readers against an erroneous impression which several of those gentlemen entertained who heard it read. I refer to the apparent meagreness of the "abstract of cases" which occurs in the Appendix. Several of my medical brethren regretted that I had not entered into symptomatic details. Nay—one went so far as to assert that a single fully delineated case would have been more useful than the 180 in the condition in which they appear. Now, the fact is, that it is simply impossible to write full details of every case, if you desire to compare numbers together; the bulk of material and the minute differences render all comparisons intensely difficult, and often impossible. Who has not felt this in our *Materia Medica?* wherein, if you attempt a minute comparison of two or more remedies, you soon land yourself in inextricable confusion, seeing there is no standard wherewith to mark the limits within which the minuter elements of a symptom may vary, without entitling it to be considered as a distinct variety. The object of this demand for the minute details of every symptom of a case, is to bring any failure which may occur to the test given by Hahnemann, in his oft-quoted challenge of 1817. "Take a case," said he, "of course one for which a homœopathic remedy has already been discovered, note down all its perceptible symptoms in the manner which has been taught in the Organon, and with a correctness with which the author of homœopathy shall be perfectly satisfied; apply that drug which shall be perfectly homœopathic to all the symptoms, the dose being of the size prescribed in the Organon, and avoiding all those heterogeneous influences which might disturb the action of the drug; and if, under these circumstances, the drug does not afford speedy and efficient help, then publish the failure to the world in a manner which shall make it impossible for me to deny the homœopathicity of the drug and the correctness of your proceedings, and the author of homœopathy will stand confounded and convicted." Four separate reasons lead me to regret, exceedingly, that the above sentence has been so often and so boastfully referred to. 1st. It ill accords with the spirit of various parts of the Organon, and especially with paragraphs 162-3 and 4, where Hahnemann speaks of the results obtained by remedies only partially homœopathic to the disease, but still more contrary does it appear to be to the instances deduced from allopathic sources, by Hahnemann, in proof of the homœopathic law, since in many of these, no such minute accordance of the symptoms is perceptible, and no reference is made to the question of dose, or the counteracting influence of mixed medication. 2d. If the terms of this challenge be accepted as the essential ground upon which the non-success of homœopathy in any case must be based, we cannot resist the conclusion, that all the so-called cures by homœopathic remedies which do not come up to this standard must be rejected, and the results taken as belonging to the large class of recoveries which take place *after* the administration of medicine, *not in consequence* thereof. 3d. I am surprised it has never occurred to those who refer to the above sentence, that if it were strictly true, homœopathy would be at once reduced to the condition of a pretty, scientific toy, possessed of no practical value whatever, since it would be impossible for any one to prescribe, in strict accordance with the rules laid down, in so far as it but seldom happens that a remedy *can be found possessing so absolute and minute a correspondence* of symptoms as is here demanded. I would like those who bandy about this challenge to weigh well the fate of the electric light, which was discovered more than thirty years ago by Sir H. Davy, and while acknowledged by all as absolutely superior to every method of illumination yet known, has hitherto baffled the efforts of our ablest mechanicians to render it available in practice—surely no well wisher of his race would desire that such a calamity should befall our glorious therapeia. 4. The challenge as it stands proves injurious to our cause, as it lays its author open to the charge of sophistry, since he has not left the materials wherewith the test can be applied; the state of our *Materia Medica*, where, from an over desire to simplify, all clue has been lost to the natural grouping of the symptoms; the discordant opinions entertained respecting the dose and its repetition; the vague ideas current as to the length of time during which a remedy sustains its action, and our almost entire ignorance as to the reciprocal influence exerted by a medicine over one subsequently administered; combine to render it impossible that any one shall so conduct a case, that another disciple of Hahnemann shall "find it impossible to deny the homœopathicity of the drug or the correctness of the proceedings."—Under these circumstances, one cannot avoid tracing a resemblance between the above challenge, and that often given by schoolboys to a new comer, to engage at "pitch and toss" under the auspicious terms of "heads I win, tails you lose."

Let it not be supposed, however, that I object altogether to minutely detailed cases, far from it, such details may prove most valuable in advancing our knowledge of therapeutics but I maintain that it is impossible to test with absolute certainty the correctness of the treatment of any case by the minute detail of symptoms alluded to in Hahnemann's challenge, and accordingly where a large number of cases of the same disease are brought under review, it is quite unnecessary to enter into each in such a manner as to individualize and separate it from the mass; besides which, the whole scope of my paper is to illustrate general principles, since any attempt at detail would have extended it altogether beyond the ordinary limits of an oral address.

My views respecting the practical working out of the homœopathic principle may be briefly stated as follows:—We must in the first place, learn to diagnose the medicines, just as we would study the diagnosis of a disease, and until we have attained such knowledge we cannot employ our remedies with confidence.

2d. As regards those maladies which evidence themselves by subjective sensations only, we cannot be too minute in the examination of details.

3d. Where objective symptoms exist, and where the actual pathological condition is detectable, we must consider a correspondence in this respect between the pathogenesis of the medicine and the disease as a question of vastly more consequence, than minute shades of difference in the subjective sensations.

4th. We shall find it of more practical value to gain acquaintance with the sphere of action of a remedy, together with its characteristic groups of symptoms and special peculiarities, than if we succeeded in retaining in our minds the whole mass of symptoms recorded in the provings.

5th. In entering into minute detail we must never forget that the power of accurate observation is very small in the vast majority of patients, and hence the grounds whereon to rest our selection, if influenced by minute shades of difference, is very insecure, and may mislead us far more than the well grounded deduction of a pathological comparison between the known action of the remedy and the ascertained condition of the patient.

APPENDIX.

ABSTRACT OF 180 CASES

OF

UTERINE DISEASES AND THEIR TREATMENT,

TOGETHER WITH ANALYTICAL TABLES OF RESULTS, AGES, SYMPTOMS, ETC.

NOTE 1. Among the 180 cases reported in the following abstract there occur one case of Cancer, (90,) and two of Scirrhus, (62, 157,) these however do not find a place in the calculations which follow, and are only introduced to show that while the two cases of Scirrhus obtained no benefit from general treatment alone, the case of Cancer was for a time decidedly relieved by local remedies in conjunction with general treatment. In the calculated tables the places of these three are supplied by (6x, 27x, 102x,) which are re-entries of the preceding cases (6, 27, 102), as the patients returned under treatment suffering from a distinctly different condition of the Uterus. These and 52x are the only instances of double entry throughout the abstract.

NOTE 2. As regards the medicines, the figures following each indicate the potency, and when the letter x is added, it denotes that the potency was according to the decimal scale—thus *Puls.* 3. denotes the 3d centesimal and *Puls.* 3x the 3d decimal potency of this remedy. The letter O denotes the mother tincture.

ABSTRACT OF ONE HUNDRED AND EIGHTY CASES,

ETC. ETC.

No.	Age.	Length of illness.	Uterine discharge.	Chief symptoms.	Length of time under treatment.	Results.	Remedies which relieved.
1	29 Single	6 or 8 months	***Menses*** scanty — no ***Leucorrhœa*** Not examined.	Weak, dyspeptic, short-breathed	9½ months	Benefitted	***Puls.*** 3x—Sulph. 3—***Calc.*** 12—***Puls.*** 6—***Nux vom.*** 12—Nux v. 6—Puls. 12—Sep. 12—***Ferrum Sulph.*** 1x—Arsen. 6 6.
2	18 Single	9 months	***Menses*** copious — much ***Leucorrhœa.*** Examined	Weak, dyspnœa, pain in back, nervous Vagina and Uterus very sensitive	7½ months	Has varied much, at times much better	Sepia 5—***Puls.*** 12—Bell. 12—Ign. 6—***Bell.*** 3x—Sepia 12—Puls. 3x.
3	21 Single	12 months	***Menses*** absent, never regular—much ***Leucorrhœa*** Not examined	Weak, severe headache	4 months	Cured. Has had relapses of headache when menses delayed	Puls. 12—***Kali carb.*** 12 12—Puls. 12—Kali carb. 6—Sepia 12 12.
4	16 Single	6 months	***Menses*** not commenced Not examined	Chlorotic, vomiting, pains in abdomen	10 months	Menses came on in fourteen weeks and continued, but with much pain at times—general health better	***Bry.*** 3x—***Puls.*** 30 30—***Sulph.*** 12 ***Sep.*** 12—***Mangan ac.*** 1—Cocculus 3—Puls. 6.
5	20 Single	6 months	***Menses*** absent—frequent ***Leucorrhœa*** Not examined	Palpitation, dyspnœa, debility, pains in back and abdomen	2 months	Some benefit	Sep. 5—Natrum mur. 12 ***Ferr. ac.*** 2.
6	15 Single	3 months	***Menses*** absent — much ***Leucorrhœa*** Not examined	A fit once a month, pain in back	2 months	Fits left her at once, menses returned, and she was well	Bell. 3 3—Sep. 5—Kali c. 3 6.

6x	15 Single		*Menses* irregular — some *Leucorrhœa* Not examined	Headache and irregular menses	4 months	Improved	Bell. 6 — Puls. 6 12—Kali c. 6—Sep. 12 12.
7	28 Single	Many years	*Menses* very scanty and painful—slight *Leucorrhœa* Examined	*Extreme debility*, nervousness, pains all over, especially in right ovary Uterus tender, but *looks* healthy	6 weeks	Not much change—was formerly under my care many months with doubtful benefit	Arsen. 30.—Bell. 3.
8	22 Single	Some years	*Menses* very scanty, too late, and painful—much *Leucorrhœa* Not examined	*Dysmenorrhœa, headache, dyspepsia*	12 months	Occasional relief, but neither great, nor permanent	Sep. 12—Puls. 6—Cocc. 3—Nux v. 3—*Graph.* 5. Bell. 3x.—*Graph.* 5.
9	25 Single	Many months	*Menses* scanty and pale—copious *Leucorrhœa* Not examined	*Leucorrhœa, Debility* (faceache,) backache	6 weeks	Improving, Leucorrhœa much better	Sulph. 12—Calc. 12.
10	18 Single	7 months	*Menses* absent—no *Leucorrhœa* Not examined	Vertigo, congestion of head, flushed face	1 month	Nearly cured, menses have returned, some nervous trembling alone remains	Acon. 3.—*Bell.* 6.
11	20 Single	2 months	*Menses* absent Not examined	*Headache*, tremulous weakness	1 month	Headache better, menses returned	Puls. 6.
12	40—50 married, a large family.	2 or 3 years	*Menses* very copious every 14 days—some *Leucorrhœa* Not examined	*Menorrhagia*, burning in back, *debility*, &c.	3½ months	Benefitted, but varied much—left the Town	Vinca *a* 1-20 Bell. 3—Plat. 3 3—Rhus. 6.
13	25 Single	6 years	*Menses* very scanty Not examined	Dysmenorrhœa, *pain in back*	3½ months	Decidedly benefitted, but left Town. I believe she had retroversion, probably requiring mechanical aid	Nux v. 3.—Bry. 12—Sep. 12—12 — Alum. 12—Berb 3.
14	25 Single	a long time	*Menses* regular — copious *Leucorrhœa* Not examined	*Languor* and *debility*, cough	18 days	Decidedly benefitted, but left the Town	Phos. 3—Sep. 6.
15	26 Single	3 years	*Menses* regular—painful Not examined	Dysmenorrhœa, *severe abdominal pain for a week before menses*	7 months	Varied much, pain ceased for 2 and 3 periods and then returned — there were many untoward moral causes in operation throughout	Carb. v. 5—*Sep.* 12.

No.	Age.	Length of illness.	Uterine Discharge.	Chief symptoms.	Length of time under treatment.	Result.	Remedies which relieved.
16	33 Single	many years	*Menses* irregular, too late, occasional *Leucorrhœa* Examined once 'TOUCHER'	*Headaches—Hypogastric pain*—Dysmenorrhœa Cervix very tender, os patent and edges soft as if excoriated	18 months	In 1846 I treated her headaches with much benefit. During the 18 months of treatment for uterine symptoms, but little benefit accrued. N. B.—This case was treated chiefly by correspondence.	Arsen. 12—Bell. 3—Puls. 3—3—Nux. v. 3—(advised Lyc. 30—Graph. 30 Sulph. 30—Calc. 30, occasionally in single doses, used for 6 weeks). Examined uterus, and ordered Douche, which was used 4 months with temporary benefit; advised Bell. 30—Kali. c. 30—Sep. 30—Bry. 30 occasionally—no change — treatment followed very irregularly.
17	33 Single	long delicate, 11 months ill	*Menses* too early, copious, *Leucorrhœa* before and after menses Examined 'TOUCHER' and 'SOUND'	*General debility* — uterus only examined shortly before she left Town Os patent, considerable engorgement of uterus	on two occasions, 2 months each time	Occasional benefit: but this case I believe decidedly required local treatment, which was not followed, from want of opportunity	Sulph. 12—Calc. 12—Nux v. 3—3—Sulph. — Nux. v. 3—3—Puls. 3—Sep. 12—*Ignat.* 3—3—Bry. 3—this attendance was chiefly for catarrhs—1849 had first severe dysentery, diarrhœa, and then uterine symptoms—Bry. 3—Arsen. 6—Sulph. 12—Ign. 3—3—3 — Lach. 12—Puls. 3—Ign. 3—Ipec. 1 ordered Douche.
18	16 Single	2 or 3 months	*Menses* too early—copious and long Not examined	*Anœmia*, debility, headache	5 weeks	Not much benefitted before leaving town but she continued the treatment and got quite well	Bell. 3—3—6 — Chin. 1 Calc. 6—6.

19	38 married, no children	many years	*Menses* absent for a time then regular—copious *Leucorrhœa* Examined and treated by Simpson's pessary	Debility and local weakness as of threatened prolapse — her general health much disordered from other causes, chiefly imperfect nutrition from irritable stomach; the treatment of the uterine symptoms was purely mechanical and perfectly satisfactory. She wore the pessary from May 14, 1849, to February 8, 1850, without any inconvenience and was cured. Anteversion and uterus engorged	9 months		
20	40 married, 1 child	2 years; since first confinement	*Menses* regular—copious—slight *Leucorrhœa* Not axamined	*Debility*, irregular and very slow action of heart. Membranous dysmenorrhœa	3½ months	No decided benefit.	Dig. 3—3—Alum. 30—Sep. 30.—Lyc. 30—Graph. 12.
21	22 Single	14 months	*Menses* too early—copious much *Leucorrhœa* Examined and treated locally with much more success than general treatment. — ARGENTI NIT. PERNIT OF MERCURY	*Debility, pain in back, Hypogastric weight.* Inflammation and ulceration of cervix and canal.	8 months	General health somewhat benefitted by the general treatment, but uterine symptoms remained unchanged till local treatment was commenced, since which she has benefitted considerably	Kali. c. 3.— 12. (menses ceased now, Jan. 3d, and did not return,) Merc. corr. 2— 2—Bry. 3x.—3x.
22	30 married, no children	12 years	*Menses* very copious—occasional *Leucorrhœa* Examined, treated by Simpson's pessary without any benefit	*Pain in back*, constipation. Retroversion and second stage of cervico-metritis	3 months	No real benefit, and the pessary appeared to do harm. I, however, lost sight of the case while she was wearing it	Sulph. O—Alum. 3.—Bry. 3.

No.	Age.	Length of illness.	Uterine Discharge.	Chief Symptoms.	Length of time under treatment.	Results.	Remedies which relieved.
23	40—50 married, 11 children. 1 miscarriage. youngest 5 years	8 years	*Menses* regular — scanty *Leucorrhœa* Examined	***General debility**, **nervous symptoms**.* Hypogastric pain. A large ulcer on cervix healed in centre, raw round edges	3½ months	Completely cured locally, and general health much improved, hysteria often returns. Local treatment consisted of douche only.	Kali Iod. 1. Mag. Carb. 6. Nux M. 6. *Kali Carb*. 3—3. *Lach*. 6.
24	33 Single	a long time	***Menses*** regular, copious—slight *Leucorrhœa* Not examined	***Debility***, neuralgic pains in back, headache, &c.	5½ months	Decided benefit to general health — many uterine symptoms return at times.	Nux v. 12. — Ign. 6 — Nux m. 3x.—Plat. 12—Plat. 12—12.—Cham. 12 —Bell. 3.
25	14 Single	some months	***Menses*** irregular Examined 'TOUCHER'	***Constipation***, disinclination for all exertion. Uterus sensitive to touch, she masturbated	9 weeks	But little benefit before she left town, but ultimately recovered under homœopathic treatment. I chiefly treated the constipation.	Puls. 3—Bry. 3—Plat. 6.
26	35 Single	many years	***Menses*** regular Examined 'SOUND,' and treated with Simpson's pessary	***Hysteria***, spinal and uterine irritation, ***constipation*** Retroversion of uterus, also uterus sensitive to touch, os patent	11 months	For some months greatly benefitted, but became worse after the use of the pessary, and returned to allœopathic treatment	Nux v. 3.—Sulph. 6.—Nux v. 6. — Puls. 6.—Sep. 12. — Bry. 3x—3x 1.—Merc. 3—Nux. v. 3s —Bry. 3x. (Oct. 17 introduced pessary) ***Chin.*** 1.—Bell. 3x. — Nux v. 3. (March 2d removed pessary) Plat. 6.—Ignat. 3x.
27	27 Single	many years	***Menses*** regular, ***Leucorrhœa*** Not examined	Hysteria, faintness, ***pain in back***, debility, &c.	6 months	Some temporary benefit	Puls. 6—Nux v. 30—Sep. 30.
27x	27 Single	many years	***Menses*** regular,—***Leucorrhœa*** Examined and treated by Simpson's pessary, and ARGENTI NIT.	Hysteria, faintness, pain in back, debility, &c. Retroversion, ulceration of cervix and canal, posterior wall engorged	1 year and 7 months	The local treatment did much good, but was given up before the cure was complete; many moral symptoms checked the progress much	Merc. 5. (***Argen. nit.*** at times from Jan. 22 to Nov. 7th) ***Kali. Iod.*** 1—***Merc. ac.*** 1—Merc. I. 1 (introduced pessary Dec. 30th, removed it Oct. 11th,)

							at one time the pessary caused much pain, but this was at once removed by re-adjusting the instrument) Lach. 6—*Merc. corr.* 2—Bry. 3—Rhus. 3x.
28	30—40 married, 4 or 5 children	some years	*Menses* always have been copious; for some time Menorrhagia Examined shortly before she left town—'TOUCHER'	*Hysteria*, great general debility. Menorrhagia, posterior wall engorged, uterus sensitive to touch, os patent	7½ months	All the usual remedies for excessive menstruation and hysteria were given in various ways, as regards potency, dose, &c., with only occasional and temporary benefit—Plat. 12—Ign. 3 and, at one time, Secale 3 did good. On examination, however, chronic inflammation of posterior wall of uterus was discovered, and I believe local remedies alone will do good. The patient left town before these were tried, but will probably return.	
29	27 married, 1 child	4 years since child-birth	*Menses* very copious and long continued, occasional *Leucorrhœa* Examined and treated by Douche and Simpson's pessary	*Menorrhagia*, debility, bearing down pain, spasmodic cough Enlargement and anteversion of uterus, os patent	2 years and 5 months	Much benefitted by pessary, after which she became pregnant, had a still-born seven months' child and has since felt weak at times, though, on the whole, decidedly better, the menses much less copious	Vinca 1. (applied pessary March 8th, and removed it July 8th,) Chin. 1—*Kali carb.* 3—Cina. 3x—Ammon. carb. 3x—Thuja. 3.—Chin. sul. 1. Ammon. carb. 3x.
30	27 married, has children	some years	*Menses* too frequent, pale, copious *Leucorrhœa* at times. Not examined	Pain in left ovarian region	3 months	Benefitted, but not cured; left too soon to judge	*Sulph.* 30.—Bell. 30.
31	20 Single	some years	*Menses* regular,—*Leucorrhœa* copious, yellow, fœtid. Examined, treated by Douche and Simpson's pessary	*Leucorrhœa*, hysteria, hepatic pain, &c. Retroversion of Uterus, and 1st stage of cervico-metritis	7½ months	Much benefit to general health, some uterine symptoms remain but much less urgent. Pessary appeared to do good and caused no inconvenience. The retroversion was completely cured	Ign. 3x.—Calc. 6.—Sulph. 12.—Bry. 3x.—*Kali c.* 3. (she wore the pessary from Dec. 30th to July 9th.)

No.	Age.	Length of illness.	Uterine discharge.	Chief symptoms.	Length of time under treatment.	Results.	Remedies which relieved.
32	30—40 married, 8 children	many years	*Menses* usually very copious — copious yellow *Leucorrhœa* Examined and found	*Hysteria*, *catalepsy*, debility, *Leucorrhœa*, &c. Ulceration (syphilitic) — uterine engorgement	2 years	Was very irregularly under treatment, never long at a time, and refused to submit to local remedies, only temporary benefit was obtained	Nit. ac. 2—Merc. 5—Rhus. 3x.
33	41 married, no children	2 years	*Menses* copious and almost constant — thick yellow copious *Leucorrhea* Examined 'TOUCHER'	*Leucorrhœa*, *Menorrhagia*, debility, pain in back Irregular induration of cervix	6½ months	Cured without local treatment. The recumbent posture was enjoined for two or three months	Chin. 6.—Arsen. 6.—Sep. 12 — Sep. 30 — *Sep.* 30.—*Aur.* 30.—Sulph. 30.—Sep. 30.
34	30—40 Single	many years	*Menses*, frequent, copious—copious *Leucorrhœa* for 8 or 9 days after menses Not examined	Debility, *Menorrhagia*, *Leucorrhœa*, an abdominal tumor which is probably fibrous tumor of Uterus	11½ months	Considerable benefit to general health, not much change in the uterine symptoms.	Sulph. 30.—Bry. 30.—Graph. 3.
35	40 married, 4 or 5 children	2 years	*Menses* copious early—occasional copious serous *Leucorrhœa* Examined, 'TOUCHER' and 'SOUND,' which caused spasm	*Numbness of right arm and leg*, debility Has had perinæum ruptured which permits of partial prolapse. *Uterus* engorged, os patent	6½ months occasional	Not much change in 1848—decided benefit in 1850	Zinc 30.—Nux v. 12.—Bry. 3x.—Nux v. 3x.
36	30—5 married, 2 children, 3 miscarriages	3 months	*Menses* irregular Examined	*Bearing down pain*, debility, is hysterical Os patent	2½ months	Cured—Very soon after examination with the "*sound*," she became pregnant and soon got well.	Bry. 3x—*Nux v.* 6 12—*Puls.* 12—*Sulph.* 6 12.—Had a healthy child, made a good recovery.
37	22 Single	a long time	*Menses* too late, painful Examined just before she went away	*Opisthotonos*, — *hysteria*, *pain in back*, debility, second stage of cervico-metritis	5½ months	Is extremely fanciful about the medicines, and every remedy produced some kind of aggravation. I only treated the fits, and without any success, except that traceable to moral causes. Dr. Bennet then took the case; detected ulceration of cervical canal, treated and healed it with caustic which did very much good. A relapse of the fits, some months after, yielded to change of air and scene. The patient however is still far from well.	

38	50 married, no children.	21 years	*Menses* have ceased—occasional *Leucorrhœa* Examined, hymen perfect	***Burning pain and tenderness in sacrum***, inability to walk far Inflammation and ulceration of cervical canal	12 months	General remedies had no effect; ARGENTI NIT. healed the excoriation and removed inflammation of cervical canal, but symptoms continue	Bry. 3x.—Kali Bichrom. 3x.
39	40—5 married, no children.	many years	*Menses* with much pain—*Leucorrhœa* Examined, 'TOUCHER.'	General debility, ***bearing down pain, constipation, dyspepsia*** Enlargement and congestion anteriorly	7 months occasional	Cured. The case progressed slowly, and went on well during her absence, when she prescribed for herself p.r.n.	Puls. 6—Sep. 30—Bell. 30—K. Bich. 2 6—Merc. acet. 3x.—Nux v. 3x.—*Arsen.* 6.
40	25 married, 1 child 2 years old.	2 years	*Menses* regular till six weeks before treatment, now absent — *Leucorrhœa* occasionally in gushes Examined	Bearing down pain after all exertion, debility Anterior wall congested and tender, lip red, not excoriated	1 month	Relieved, but left the town too soon to judge the effect of treatment. Sea water douche used	Sepia 12.
41	21 Single	3 or 4 years	*Menses* never free, too late, absent, pale or brown—copious *Leucorrhœa* Not examined	*Leucorrhœa*, pain across top of thighs, easily fatigued	1 month	Much improved, but left town too soon to judge. Menses occurred once, more healthily, she used cold sitz bath and abdominal compress occasionally	*Sulph.* 12.
42	35 married, child 7 years old.	many years, worse 18 months.	*Menses* regular Examined once, 'TOUCHER' and 'SOUND'	*Great debility*, discharge of pus per anum, has evidently pelvic abscess, which showed itself after the use of Simpson's pessary, but probably existed previously Retroflection	4 months	A little improvement to general health, varied much	Silic. 6—Puls. 6—China 3.

No.	Age.	Length of illness.	Uterine dischage.	Chief symptoms.	Length of time under treatment.	Results.	Remedies which relieved.
43	18 Single	some time	*Menses* too frequent, scanty, and painful—copious *Leucorrhœa* Not examined	*Leucorrhœa*, pain in left side, pain in back	6 weeks	Very much improved, but left too early to be cured	Nux v. 12—*Sep.* 12—*Sulph.* 6.
44	18 Single	3 years	*Menses* regular, scanty, and very dark—copious *Leucorrhœa* Not examined	*Nervous debility extreme*, Severe left side pain, &c. Bearing down pain.	6 months	No improvement of any duration; this case should have been examined, and most likely required local treatment.	
45	35—40 married several childr'n	a long time ill	*Menses* very copious and frequent — *Leucorrhœa* copious Not examined	*Menorrhagia*, vomiting, pain in left side	4½ months	Cured	Sep. 12—Bell. 6—Carb. v. 30—*Alum.* 30—Cham. 30—Alum. 30—Graph. 30.
46	30—5 Single	11 years	*Menses* pretty regular, painful—occasional *Leucorrhœa* Examined, treated by Douche, Simpson's pessary, and Argenti Nit.	*Pains in back and groins, great debility, headache,* retroversion of uterus. Inflammation and ulceration of cervical canal—engorgement of posterior wall	2 years 4 months	A very instructive case, general remedies did no permanent good; neither did the douche; Simpson's pessary did fully more harm than good, though it removed the retroversion. But when Argenti Nit. was freely applied to the cervical canal, improvement commenced and progressed satisfactorily, though not rapidly—Bell. 3x. Hyper. 3x. relieved the headache. No remedy was of marked use, but many relieved.	
47	27 married 1 child 5 m'ths	5 months	*Menses* absent, is suckling—copious *Leucorrhœa* Not examined	Pain in left side, *Leucorrhœa*, sinking at epigastrium	2 months	Cured	Acon. 6—*Sulph.* 30—*Nux v.* 30.
48	20 Single	3 years	*Menses* too late—some *Leucorrhœa*. Not examined	*Headache*, — occasional nausea	1 month	Cured. Relieved from a relapse, and she then left the town	Puls. 3—*Puls.* 6—*Puls.* 12—Bell. 6.
49	18 Single	3 months	*Menses* absent Not examined	*Amenorrhœa*,—*headache*, dyspepsia, pain in loins	6 months	At first relief to general health, then no further improvement. Menses did not return. Widow Welch's pills cured her soon after she left my charge	Bell. (only high potencies, and at long intervals, were tried)

50	24 Single	6 months	*Menses* absent 12 months—no *Leucorrhœa* Not examined	*Headache*, *Amenorrhœa*, nausea	6 months	No marked improvement, and no return of menses	Low potencies hiefly were tried.
51	44 married, 3 children	16 months	*Menses* copious every 14 days—occasional *Leucorrhœa*. Not examined	*Menorrhagia*, debility	17 months	General health quite restored, menses continued copious till near end of treatment	Puls. 6—Plat. 6—Arsen. 12.
52	38 married, several children	some time	*Menses* regular—copious *Leucorrhœa* Examined, treated by ARGENTI NIT.	*Leucorrhœa*, debility, pain in abdomen Os irregular and patent, cervix ulcerated	6½ months	Cured, and continued well until after another confinement, when uterine symptoms returned—see 52x	ARGENTI NIT. locally had most effect, Merc. c. 2—Lach. 6.
52x			*Menses* regular—copious *Leucorrhœa* Not examined	*Leucorrhœa*, debility, pain in abdomen	10 weeks	Cured	Bell. 2x.
53	28 Single	4 years	*Menses* absent, or very scanty Examined 'TOUCHER' and 'SOUND'	*Chlorosis*, debility, cardiac pain, and breathlessness *Uterus* low down, os patent and irregular	12 months	No permanent benefit—probably the speculum would have revealed local disease	Plumb. 12—Graph. 30. Nux v. 30.
54	23 married, 1 child	2 months	*Menses* absent, is nursing. *Leucorrhœa* Examined and treated by ARGENTI NIT.	Debility, pain in left side Ulceration of cervix uteri	3 or 4 months	Cured locally. This patient had threatened phthisis for years, the ulceration followed a miscarriage, and was cured by ARGENTI NIT. She again became pregnant, and had a healthy child, after which she had no return of uterine symptoms but sank from phthisis.	
55	28 Single	12 years	*Menses* regular, painful, occasional *Leucorrhœa* Examined after 7 months' unsuccessful general treatment—ARGENTI NIT.	*Headache*, *pain in right side*, debility Inflammation of cervical canal	17 months	Not any relief till after I commenced local treatment, in March, 1850, since which she has progressed slightly, and is still under treatment. After examination, in September, the douche was tried, without benefit.	
56	23 Single	some time	*Menses* scanty, pale, painful—*Leucorrhœa* Not examined	*Dysmenorrhœa*, pain in loins	5 months	General health restored, menses were better and less painful, but just before I lost sight of her they passed their time	*Puls.* 6—*Sulph.* 12—*Puls.* 6.
57	20 Single	9 weeks	*Menses* absent Not examined	Amenorrhœa	8 days	Cured	*Puls.* 6 (no other remedy).

No.	Age.	Length of illness.	Uterine discharge.	Chief symptoms.	Length of time under treatment.	Results.	Remedies which relieved.
58	50 married	2 years	*Menses* constant, pale discharge—query, was not this *Leucorrhœa?* Not examined.	*Nervousness*, occasional fits, apparently epileptic	6 weeks	General health improved, fits less frequent, and was then lost sight of	Lach. 12—Bell. 12.
59	35 Single	3 months	*Menses*, scanty and pale—*Leucorrhœa* Not examined	*Pain in loins and hypogastrium*	5 months	Cured; but when the uterine symptoms ceased pectoral ones supervened, which lasted nine months. No local remedies were used.	Sulph. 6—Puls. 6—Graph. 6—Bell. 6—*Ferr.* 6—Sep. 30.
60	30 married no children	8 years	*Menses*, too copious and too frequent, *Leucorrhœa* Not examined	*Headache*, dysmenorrhœa, bearing down pain	3 months	No permanent relief (this case should have been examined and probably treated locally)	Ign. 3—Cocculus 6.
61	16 Single	5 or 6 months	*Menses* absent 7 months, have only occurred twice Not examined	*Pain in left side and epigastrium*, dyspepsia	3 months	Health restored; menses did not re-appear	Puls. 6—Puls. 3—Bell. 3 *Puls.* 3—Kali c. 3.
62	53 married	4 months	*Menses* constant, sanguineous discharge Examined 'TOUCHER'	*The discharge*, great debility Posterior wall of uterus *very hard*, scirrhus?	5 weeks	No change, no local remedies were used. She went into the hospital	
63	67 married	many years	Not examined	Prolapse of uterus and rectum, some *abdominal* pain	2 months	Pain removed, no local improvement	Sepia 5—Sulph. O.
64	17 Single	some time	*Menses* regular, not much pain, pale—slight *Leucorrhœa* Not examined	Hysteria, debility, dyspepsia, &c.	19 months	Only occasionally under treatment, and was at times much better. After May, 1849, she became worse; dysmenorrhœa and convulsions came on, which were treated locally by Dr. Simpson, and, 'by report' cured	Puls. 3—Nux v. 6—Lach. 6—Carbo v. 5—Car. v. 5 12 30—*Graph.* 5 12 30—*Calc.* 3 12 30—Puls. 6 12 30.

65	30 married, no children	some time	*Menses* very painful, and with false membrane Not examined	*Dysmenorrhœa*, debility, hysteria	10 months	Conducted chiefly by correspondence, and not regularly; no marked benefit. She is at present (1850) under Dr. Blake's cure and is improving, headache at times much relieved	Canth. 3—*Secale* 6—*Secale* 6
66	18 Single	11 months	*Menses* absent 11 months, occasional *Leucorrhœa* Not examined	*Amenorrhœa*, Chlorosis, Cardiac symptoms	4 months	Menses occurred once scantily and then again ceased—general health improved considerably. She worked too hard at her needle	Sep. 12—Puls. 6—Graph. 6—Puls. 6—Puls. 6
67	29 married, 5 children	4 or 5 months	Is pregnant—copious *Leucorrhœa*, yellow Not examined	*Leucorrhœa*, pain in loins, hypogastric pain	3 months	Improvement in health, Leucorrhœa continued, though less in quantity—left too soon to judge	Sulph. 30—Sepia 30—*Sepia* 30
68	39 married	12 months	*Menses* regular and very copious — copious *Leucorrhœa*, yellow Not examined	*Gastrodynia*, headache, *Leucorrhœa*	6 weeks	Dyspeptic symptoms cured. Uterine symptoms not mentioned in last two reports	*Puls.* 6
69	38 married, 3 children, youngest 7	12 months	*Menses* regular, very scanty—copious white *Leucorrhœa* Not examined	*Leucorrhœa*, pain in loins, debility, frequent micturition.	3½ months	Not much benefit	Calc. 30—Sulph. 30—Calc. 30—Sep. 12
70	25 Single	2 years	*Menses* absent two years, some *Leucorrhœa* Examined, 'TOUCHER' and 'SOUND'	*Pain in hypochondria*, *headache*, pain in back. Nothing detected, except os and cervix unusually small and soft.	2½ months	Some benefit. No return of menses. Left the town.	Sep. 5—Puls. 3x.—Sulph. 12—Nat. m. 6.
71	17 Single	some time	*Menses* too seldom, copious—much *Leucorrhœa* Not examined	*Pain in epigastrium* and over abdomen, *pain in Hypogastrium*	3 months	Very much benefitted	Puls. 3x.—*Sep.* 5—Sep. 12—*Sulph.* 6.
72	25 Single	some months	*Menses* regular, pale, and watery—much *Leucorrhœa* Not examined	*Dyspepsia*, pain in back, debility, constipation	6 weeks	Very irregular in her attendance—not much benefitted, left town too soon	Nux v. 3.

No.	Age.	Length of illness.	Uterine discharge.	Chief symptoms.	Length of time under treatment.	Results.	Remedies which relieved.
73	30—5 Single	17 years	*Menses* pretty regular—some *Leucorrhœa* Examined, and treated by douche and Simpson's pessary	*Hæmorrhage from rectum, weight in hypogastrium*, general debility Retroversion of uterus—*uterus* engorged, os patent	23 months	Greatly benefitted. Uterine symptoms cured, though the retroflexion was not; general health greatly restored. The pessary produced much irritation and had to be removed, after wearing it from Oct. 24th to Feb. 13th—3½ months	Lach. 6—Nux v. 3x.—Lyc. 5—Natrum m. 6—Lyc. 5—*Sep.* 3x.—Puls. 3x.—Kali i. 1—Merc. a. 1—*Kreos.* 2—Nitr. ac. 2—Chin.s. 1—Ign. 3x. Ars. 3—*Bry.* 3x.—Nux v. 3
74	18 Single	2 years	*Menses* very irregular, often absent—occasional *Leucorrhœa* Not examined	*Chlorosis*, cardiac symptoms, vomiting, and much dyspepsia, with much gastralgia	5 years	Has repeatedly been under my care, and is on the whole very much better, at times much relieved—but she sits too close to needlework, and is thus subject to relapses.	Dig. 6—Sep. 30—*Puls.* 30
75	55 married	2 years	*Menses* ceased — copious yellow *Leucorrhœa* Not examined	*Leucorrhœa*	1 month	No change — Medicine (Sep.) made her constantly drowsy all day long, which she had never been before.	
76	26 Single	2 years	*Menses* regular, scanty, painful—thick corrosive *Leucorrhœa* Not examined	*Pain in abdomen*, pus per anum at times	2 months	Greatly benefitted, but did not attend regularly.—Leucorrhœa became less	Sulph. 12—Calcar. 18.
77	18 Single	8 months	*Menses* absent 8 months Not examined	Headache, nervousness, fear of becoming deranged	4½ months	Cured. It is not stated whether menses returned	Bell. 3—*Ign.* 6.
78	19 Single	a long time	*Menses* too frequent, long, and copious—some *Leucorrhœa* Not examined	*Headache*, debility	6 weeks	*Menses* became more regular and normal, headache continued bad and she was removed by her friends into the hospital	Calc. a. 3
79	26 Single	some months	*Menses* very scanty and pale—some *Leucorrhœa* Not examined	Palpitation, cardiac bruit, chlorosis and debility	3½ months	No marked improvement; she was constantly overworked at her needle, and confined to the house	Low potencies were used, except at the two last visits, when Sep. 30 was given with slight benefit

80	22 Single	a long time	*Menses* absent 4 or 5 months Not examined	Constipation, swelled legs, headache	2½ months	Much relieved, menses occurred once, and then again passed their time, just before I lost sight of the case	Puls. 3—1.
81	35 Single	many years	*Menses* very often absent —occasional *Leucorrhœa* Examined, treated with ARGENTI NIT.	Many symptoms, debility, *pain in back, &c.* Great distension of abdomen, inflammation of cavity of cervix	5½ months	This patient evidently suffers from many other symptoms besides the uterine ones; the latter did not yield until local treatment was used which *completely cured* them, and, for a time, benefitted the general health	Bell. 3x. — Puls. 3x. — Lach. 6—Sep. 6—Plumb. a. 1.
82	25 Single	9 months	*Menses* very scanty and pale — occasional *Leucorrhœa* Not examined	*Pain in left side*, general debility	3½ months	Much benefitted; lost sight of before she was well. Menses continued pale and scanty, Leucorrhœa decreased	*Graph.* 30 –*Graph.* 6 30.
83	25 married, no children	2 years	*Menses*, condition not stated Examined 'TOUCHER' and 'SOUND'	*Hypogastric weight*, pain in left iliac region, vertical headache Vagina, os and cervix very tender, uterus slightly retroflexed, os patent	only seen occasionally	This case has only been treated by medicine, and has varied much, is evidently not yet *cured*.—July, 1850	
84	. 33 Single	15 years	*Menses* regular — occasional *Leucorrhœa* Examined, and treated by 'SOUND.'	General health bad, has diseased ears, &c., &c., in addition to uterine symptoms, these are chiefly dysmenorrhœa, hysteria, &c. Retroflexion, uterus engorged, os somewhat patent	5½ months	Was treated by medicine alone, from Dec., 1845, to Jan., 1848, with but little real benefit, then examined, and treated by frequent introduction of SOUND. Her general health improved, uterus became less retroflexed; she married and soon became pregnant, and had a healthy child, and afterwards no uterine symptoms	The medicines did not influence the uterus at all

No.	Age.	Length of illness.	Uterine discharge.	Chief symptoms.	Length of time under treatment.	Results.	Remedies which relieved.
85	35 married, 3 children, youngest 7	8 or 10 years	*Menses* every three weeks—much *Leucorrhœa* Examined once	*Hypogastric pain, and bearing down*, great debility, *headache* Enlargement and irregularity of os	6 months	Not much benefitted	Nux v. 6—Nux v. 3—(state of uterus at close of treatment not known).
86	21 Single	a long time	*Menses* regular, very pale Examined 'TOUCHER'	*Great weakness, hysteria, palpitation*, bearing down pain, &c. Cervix uteri elongated, tender (inflamed?)	13½ months	On the whole she felt much better, but continued far from well; she subsequently married and had children, and continued delicate	Puls. 12—Lach. 30—Puls. 30—Sep. 30—Bell. 3—Puls. 3—Merc. 5.
87	25 Single	several years	*Menses* irregular, often absent, scanty, and pale *Leucorrhœa* before menses Not examined	*Headache*, debility, nausea, &c.	2½ months	General health much improved; *menses* did not become regular, her attendance was very irregular	Merc. 6—Arsen. 12—(Silic. 6).
88	27 married, 1 child, 14 months	14 months	*Menses* regular, too short—*Leucorrhœa* Examined and treated by ARGENTI NIT.	*Bearing down pain, Leucorrhœa*, debility Ulceration of os	4½ months	Ulceration completely cured and health much improved, she, however, frequently caught cold and thus retarded her progress	Merc. iod. 3x.—*Chin.* 1.
89	25 Single	12 months	*Menses* scanty, regular, and pale—constant *Leucorrhœa* Not examined	Pain in sacrum, much dyspepsia	6 weeks	Greatly benefitted	Sep. 5—Tr. Sulph. O—*Bell.* 3
90	40 married, many children	2 or 3 years	*Menses* copious, and too frequent—copious *Leucorrhœa* Examined, and treated by PERNITR. HYDR. and POTASSA FUSA	Cachexia, debility, severe uterine pains Fungoid cancer of the uterus	1 year	*Died.* The caustics relieved for a time, she rallied much; the cancer then increased more rapidly, and with it her strength gave way	Nux v. 3—Ars. 3—Bry. 3—3x.—Bell. 3x.—Lach. 6—Ars. 2.—Con. 1—Iod. 2.

91	36 married, 5 children, youngest 6	7 years	*Menses* regular, painful, copious and brown—milky *Leucorrhœa* Examined, and treated by Argenti Nit. and Pernitr. Hydr.	Spinal disease, aching pain in loins Ulceration of os, enlargement and hardness of cervix	8¾ months	Uterus cured; general health improved for a time, but the symptoms were chiefly spinal, and remained pretty much as before. Ulcer was cured in 4 months	Merc. c. 2—Nux v. 3x.—Merc. Iod. 3x.
92	25 married, no children	4 years, since a miscarriage	*Menses* copious, too long, dark—occasional *Leucorrhœa* Examined, treated by Argenti Nit., Potassa Fusa	(Gonorrhœa) *pain in left side of abdomen, dysmenorrhœa* Enlargement of anterior lip of uterus, os patent, canal excoriated	4 years	Uterus was not examined till 2 years after treatment commenced, previously her health improved much at times, and the gonorrhœa cured; for 1 year more, the case was treated by medicine only, with the same effect of temporary improvement. Caustics were then used repeatedly and the uterus improved, as also general health. She is, however, still delicate, and has laterodynia	Puls. 6—Calc. 12—Bry. 6—Sep. 12—Bell. 6—Lach. 6—Ammon. c. 5—*Merc. c.* 2—*Merc. a.* 3x.—Amm. c. 3x.—Bell. 2.
93	22 Single	4 years	*Menses* very scanty and painful—much *Leucorrhœa* Not examined	Debility, headache, pain in left side, bearing down	7 weeks	Much relieved; treatment was not continued long enough	Sep. 5—Puls. 3—Puls. 6
94	21 Single	4 years	*Menses* very copious every three weeks — much *Leucorrhœa* Not examined	*Menorrhagia*, anœmia, debility	15 months	Menorrhagia cured and amenorrhœa came on; health varied, was better at times, latterly less well	Sep. 12—Bell. 6—Bell. 6—Plat. 6—Plat. 6—Bell. 18—Puls. 6—Bell. 30—Calc. 30
95	30 married, 2 children	2¾ yrs. since last child	*Menses* every 14 days, copious — much *Leucorrhœa* Examined and treated locally, Argenti Nit. Kali Bichrom.	*Menorrhagia*, debility, sinking in epigastrium Inflammation and ulceration of cervix and canal	10 months	Greatly improved; local remedies were commenced after 7 months, prior to which local symptoms had improved	Ignat. 3x.—Bell. 3x.—Bry. 3x—Puls. 3x.—Sabina 3x.—Kali B. 3x.—Plat. Chl. 3—*Stann.* 3x.

No.	Age.	Length of illness.	Uterine discharge.	Chief symptoms.	Length of time under treatment.	Results.	Remedies which relieved.
96	31 Single	a long time	*Menses* never regular, often absent — ***Leucorrhœa*** Not examined	*Amenorrhœa*, dyspepsia, eruption on face	4½ months	Greatly improved in health —only one slight appearance of menses	Sulph. 30—Calc. 30—Bell. 12—Nux v. 30
97	35 married, no children.	some years	*Menses* often too frequent and copious — frequent *Leucorrhœa* Examined after 2 years, douche and mercurial balls—no effect	*Pain in epigastrium* and groin, hysteria, &c., &c., rheumatism, &c. Engorgement of uterus, frequent large discharge of pus, as if from pelvic abscess, bursting into vagina	3½ years	Has been under my care for various causes, and is always relieved by medicine, but the uterine symptoms have benefitted but little, though she has varied much. Uterine symptoms have benefitted chiefly from	Tr. Sulph. O—Merc. 5—Amm. c. 3—Kreos. 3x.
98	24 Single	5 years	*Menses* irregular, copious, and dark—copious *Leucorrhœa* Not examined	Hysteria, fainting, cardiac symptoms, dysmenorrhœa, &c.	14 months	Very much benefitted, was not regular in her attendance	Puls. 6—Ars. 12—Puls. 12—*Puls.* 30—*Ars.* 30—Sulph. 30—Calcar. 30—China. 30—Sep. 30—Sulph. 30—Bell. 30—Ferr. 12—Sep. 30—*Ferr.* 2.
99	22 Single	6 months	*Menses* regular, painful—much *Leucorrhœa* Not examined	Pain in stomach and abdomen, left side pain, *palpitation*, headache	2½ months	General health benefitted, less *Leucorrhœa;* still dysmenorrhœa, and menses scanty and pale	Nux v. 3—Puls. 3—Tr. Sulph. O.
100	16 Single	12 months	*Menses* absent 7 months Not examined	Chlorosis, left side headache	6 weeks	Menses came on and general health much improved—lost sight of	Puls. 3—***Puls.*** 12—Merc. 6
101	23 married, 1 child	5 years	*Menses* regular, copious, dark, painful — copious *Leucorrhœa* Examined 'TOUCHER'	*Dysmenorrhœa* most severe, hysteria Engorgement, os and cervix rather hard	2 years and 3½ months	Only occasionally and for a short time under treatment; the dysmenorrhœa was *cured*, but returned now and then under the influence of excitement, &c.	***Tr. Sulph.*** O—Cocc. 3

102	35 married, 2 or 3 children	3 months	*Menses* violent and copious, and too long Not examined	Menorrhagia from congested uterus	3 months	Cured	Puls. 3—China O.
102x	35 married, 2 or 3 children		*Menses* too seldom—painful—*Leucorrhœa* Examined Argenti Nit.	Bearing down pain, debility Enlargement, induration, and ulceration of cervix	5½ months	Much benefitted, left off treatment before she was well	Sep. 30—Bry. 3—3x.—Puls. 3x.
103	30 married, no children	some time	*Menses* regular — much *Leucorrhœa* Examined and treated with Scofield's pessary	Pain in back and side, and across abdomen Enlargement and chronic inflammation of uterus	5½ months	General health greatly improved; she continued to wear the pessary for some months after discontinuing her medicine, and has since felt well	*Bell.* 1—Nux v. 3—*T. Sulph.* O—*Rhus.* 3x.—Lyc. 5.
104	15 Single	9 months	*Menses* absent 9 months Not examined	Amenorrhœa, debility	7½ months	Only seen occasionally; menses returned twice, but did not continue regular	Sep. 12—Sulph. 12.
105	18 Single	5 or 6 months	*Menses* too frequent, copious, dark—much *Leucorrhœa* Not examined	Debility, palpitation, dyspepsia, &c.	3½ months	Cured; state of menses and leucorrhœa not mentioned at end of treatment	Calc. 30—Sulph. 30—Calc. 30—Sulph. 30.
106	30—5 married, no children.	3 years	*Menses* regular and painful—much yellow *Leucorrhœa* Examined—douche	*Leucorrhœa*, pains in genitals after all exertion Had gonorrhœa, and now chronic inflammation of vagina	6 months	Cured	*Merc. c.* 2—Bell. 3x.—Sep. 12.
107	35 married, 6 children.	some time	*Menses* copious, too early Examined—'douche'	Pain in abdomen and back, bearing down, debility, &c. Enlargement of uterus with endometritis	3 months	Had been treated by caustics, before coming to me, and pronounced *cured*, but still suffered much—general health improved greatly	Bry. 3x.—*Nux v.* 3x.—*Bry.* 3x.
108	18 Single	3 years	*Menses* never regular, now 9 months absent Not examined	Amenorrhœa, debility, faintness, depression	4½ months	Health restored, menses did not return	*Puls.* 3—*Sulph.* 12—Graph. 12—Puls. 30.

No.	Age.	Length of illness.	Uterine discharge.	Chief symptoms.	Length of time under treatment.	Results.	Remedies which relieved.
109	16 Single pregnant	2 years	*Menses* never regular, absent five months—*Leucorrhœa* Examined—ARGENTI NIT.	Dyspeptic and nervous symptoms Ulceration of cervix	7 weeks	This poor girl had been seduced and was pregnant, suffered much morally. The ARGENTI NIT. greatly benefitted the ulcer, but she left the town before she was cured.	Merc. iod. 3x.—Puls. 3.
110	35—40 married, a large family.	many years	*Menses* regular Examined	Hysteria, debility, pain in back, &c., headache Cervix enlarged, os patent and irregular	at intervals only	A very complicated case; long ill; treated 3 years homœopathically with some benefit. Dr. Ashwell then found ulceration of os and cervix, which he treated with ARGENTI NIT. and healed. Her system had become very susceptible by the strict hygienic rules she had followed, and she gradually and steadily became worse in health, all medicines appearing to aggravate, till at length she became deranged, and was then treated Allopathically by stimulants and tonics with decided but temporary benefit.	
111	18 Single	2 or 3 months	*Menses* absent 3 months Not examined	Amenorrhœa, Dyspepsia, throbbing of carotids	2½ months	Menses returned — health improved much—throbbing of carotids continued	Bell. 12—Bar. c. 6.
112	35 married, 3 children	many years	*Menses* scanty, dark—thick *Leucorrhœa* Examined 'TOUCHER'	Hysteria, toothache, aphthæ, &c., pains in various places Cervix enlarged, os irregular	1 year and 10 months	Symptoms often temporarily relieved, but the general features of the case remained unchanged; she was however constantly transgressing our rules, and moral causes were in continued counter-operation.	
113	30—5 married, 1 child.	3 years	*Menses* copious, clotted—*Leucorrhœa* Not examined	*Debility*, *Leucorrhœa*, pain in back	1 year	General health much improved, but she became pregnant, and aborted (afterwards became pregnant, and had a healthy child, and continued to improve under Dr. Black's care)	Puls. 12—Kreos. 12—Puls. 12—Car. v. 12—Zinc. 6—Sep. 30—Graph. 30—Puls. 30.

114	30—5 Single	some time	*Menses* copious—*Leucorrhœa* Not examined	Pain in back, debility, *Leucorrhœa*	2½ years occasionally only	Is over-worked as a daily governess; much relieved at times, but the symptoms occasionally returned	Sep. 12—Tr. Sulph. O—Sulph. 30—*Plat.* 12—*Bry. a.* 1-20th
115	21 married, 2 children	2 or 3 months	*Menses* regular—*Leucorrhœa* Not examined	Pain in side, flatulence, dyspepsia	1 month	Much improved, but lost sight of	Carb. v. 12—Cham. 6—*Lach.* 12—*Carb. v.* 12.
116	35—40 married, no children	8 or 10 years	*Menses* regular—not much *Leucorrhœa* Examined, treated mechanically	Bearing down pain, pain in back, debility, hysteria, &c. Retroversion of uterus and chronic inflammation, engorgement	5½ months	General symptoms improved, and but for moral causes would have done so much more. Dr. P. Smith afterwards restored the uterus and relieved her much by Simpson's pessary, but she still remained weak. No remedy seemed to influence the uterine symptoms.	
117	35 Single	many years	*Menses* regular—constant *Leucorrhœa* Not examined	Neuralgia, chiefly of face and head, headache, bearing down pain, great debility, constipation	15 months	No great benefit, though at times relieved. This case I believe to have been one in which the uterine symptoms were the most important, and where local treatment would probably have done good.	
118	19 Single	some time	*Menses* irregular absent 6 months Not examined	Headache, pain in hypochondria	6½ months	Cured	Puls. 6—Sulph 30—Sep. 30—Lyc. 30 (menses returned)—Tr. Sulph. O—Bell. 3—Tr. *Sulph.* O—*Bell.* 3.
119	30 married, 1 child 10 months	10 months	*Menses* every 14 days, copious—much *Leucorrhœa* Examined—Argenti Nit.	Weakness in Epigastrium, pain between shoulders, bearing down pain, debility Inflammation and ulceration of cervix	5½ months	Improved, general health better; ulcer more healthy and smaller, from Argenti Nit.; she attended irregularly, and was lost sight of	*Ign.* 3—Nux v. 3x.
120	36 married, 7 children, youngest 7	8 years	*Menses* every three weeks—*Leucorrhœa* Examined—Argenti Nit. Kali Bichrom., &c.	Irritation of bladder, dysuria, pain in back, debility Ulceration of cervix	13 months	Health improved, and dysuria became less before local treatment commenced, has progressed more rapidly since, and is still under treatment	Bry. 3x.—Tr. Sulph. O—*Nux v.* 3x.
121	58 married, 9 children, youngest 14	12 years	*Menses* ceased two years—occasional *Leucorrhœa* Examined—Argenti Nit. douche	Debility, heat in lower belly, dysuria, right hand and leg feel numb Enlargement and ulceration of cervix	7 months	General health improved; ulcer greatly benefitted by Argenti Nit., but not healed, local symptoms much relieved (subsequently had cancer mammæ)	Lach. 6—Puls. 3—Merc. c. 2—Merc. Iod. 1—Tr. Sulph. O—Bell. 3x.

No.	Age.	Length of illness.	Uterine Discharge.	Chief Symptoms.	Length of time under treatment.	Results.	Remedies which relieved.
122	51 married,	7 months	*Menses* leaving her, at times flooding—copious *Leucorrhœa*	Pain in hepatic region, varicose veins, flooding at times	8 months	Greatly improved, at times felt almost well, but was often thrown back by return of copious menses	*Bry.* 3x.—Bell. 3x.—Bell. 3x.
			Not examined				
123	18 Single	2 or 3 years	*Menses* never regular, often absent	Dyspepsia, debility, constipation, pain in left side	2 months	*Cured.* Menses became regular; she was not, however, robust	Puls. 3—Merc. 3—*Con.* 3—*Puls.* 3.
			Not examined				
124	14 Single	a few weeks	*Menses* have stopped—have only occurred three times	Eruption of head, swelled glands, amenorrhœa	2 months	Cured. State of menses not reported	*Lyc.* 12—*Lyc.* 30.
			Not examined				
125	24 Single	7 years	*Menses* irregular, pale, and scanty, often absent	Pain in left side of abdomen, and swelling	2¼ months	Much relieved, and went to service; menses continued absent	Puls. 30—Sulph. 30—Sep. 30.
			Not examined				
126	23 married, 4 children	5 months	*Menses* absent 5 months—much yellow *Leucorrhœa*	*Severe pain in left hypochondrium*, dyspepsia, debility	14 days	Relieved decidedly, and lost sight of. Menses not reported at last visit	Bell. 6—Nux v. 6.
			Not examined				
127	30 Single	4 or 5 months	*Menses* regular, scanty and too short—occasional *Leucorrhœa*	Bearing down pain, pain in back, debility	3 months	Much better, still under treatment. She however did not improve until ARGENTI NIT. was used	
			Examined—ARGENTI NIT.	Inflammation and excoriation of cervical canal			
128	30—5 Single	Some years	*Menses* regular, painful	Headache, hysteria, debility, bearing down pain, &c.	3 years and 2 months	Greatly benefitted in general health, often well for months together, but liable to relapses; at length, Dr. Ashwell saw her, pronounced the existence of chronic inflammation, and used caustics with reported benefit	Ars. 30—*Puls.* 12—*Ars.* 30—*Sulph.* 30—*Graph.* 30—Car. v. 30—Arsen. 30.
			Examined 'TOUCHER' shortly before she left me	Cervix uteri shortened and enlarged			

129	30—5 Single	many years	*Menses* very copious and debilitating Not examined	Debility, pain in back, headache, &c.	2 yrs. and 9 months occasionally	Greatly benefitted, menses regular and normal, much stronger, but does not become quite strong	Nux v. 3—Sep. 30—Sulph. 12—Alum. 30—*Bry.* 30 *Alum* 30—Plat. 6 30—Natrum m. 3.
130	21 Single	10 weeks	*Menses* absent 10 weeks Not examined	Amenorrhœa, toothache, headache	2½ months	Menses returned, but did not continue regular; health improved greatly, attendance irregular	*Puls.* 3.
131	7 Single	some time	Thick yellow *Leucorrhœa* Examined externally	*Leucorrhœa*	7 weeks	Cured	Puls. 3—*Calc. acet.* 3—*Merc. c.* 2.
132	32 married, 2 children	2½ years	*Menses* regular — copious yellow *Leucorrhœa* Examined once, used ARGENTI NIT. slightly	*Leucorrhœa*, hypogastric pain, debility Cervix enlarged, irregular, indurated and excoriated	5 months	Uterus cured; general health improved greatly, but over-fatigue and moral causes prevented complete recovery	*Nux v.* 3x.
133	18 Single	3 years	*Menses* irregular, dark, painful — copious *Leucorrhœa* Examined, once 'TOUCHER'	*Palpitation*, weakness, nervousness Uterus tender to the touch	2 months	Benefitted, leucorrhœa ceased, but left town too soon to judge.	Puls. 3—Puls. 30—Phos. 30—Tr. Sulph. O.
134	17 Single	5 months	*Menses* absent — *Leucorrhœa* Not examined	*Amenorrhœa*, debility, pain in back, swelled feet, headache, &c.	1 month	Cured	Puls. 3—Puls. 3—Sulph. 6 *Puls.* 6—*Sulph.* 6
135	21 married, 3 children, youngest 4 months	4 months	*Menses* occur slightly, but she is nursing — much *Leucorrhœa* Not examined	Debility, sinking in epigastrium, dyspepsia, *constipation*, headache	2½ months	Cured (a change to the country did good)	Carb. v. 30—Ignat. 6
136	33 Single	6 years	*Menses* regular and scanty —occasional *Leucorrhœa* Not examined	Debility, *severe pain in back* after all exertion	5 months	Very much relieved; is still under treatment, had she been more cautious she would have been well	*Bry.* 3x.—Puls. 3x.
137	21 Single	3 years	*Menses* too late, scanty, and pale, copious *Leucorrhœa* Not examined	Languor, palpitation, *pain in left side*, short breath	2 months	Very much better, left treatment too soon; menses more healthy, leucorrhœa ceased	Sep. 5—Puls. 3—Bell. 3—Tr. Sulph. O—Sulph. 30

No.	Age	Length of illness.	Uterine discharge.	Chief symptoms.	Length of time under treatment.	Results.	Remedies which relieved.
138	16 Single	3 months	*Menses* absent 3 months Not examined	*Pain in left side*, chlorosis, palpitation, headache	3 months	*Menses* returned, felt better at times, still had pain in side; left treatment too soon	Puls. 3—Kali c. 3—Lach. 6.
139	25 Single	2 years	*Menses* irregular, scanty, and pale Not examined	*Irregular menstruation*, headache, nausea, pain in thighs	1 month	Felt quite well for some months, then became dyspeptic, without menstrual irregularity, and was again much benefitted	Sep. 6—Puls. 6—Bell. 6 Puls. 6.
140	24 married, 3 children. youngest 6 weeks.	6 weeks	*Menses* absent, is nursing—copious *Leucorrhœa* Not examined	*Pain in left iliac region*, *leucorrhœa*, debility, dyspepsia, &c.	2½ months	Very much relieved; leucorrhœa greatly diminished	Sab. 6—*Sab.* 6 Several remedies as Sulph. 30—Sep. 30—Bell. 30—Puls. 30 were previously given without any benefit.
141	22 Single	6 months	*Menses* absent 6 months Not examined	Pain in left side of chest, dyspepsia, debility, &c.	4 months	*Menses* returned, health greatly improved	Ars. 30—Sep. 30—*Merc.* 3—*Puls.* 3.
142	29 Single	several months	*Menses* every 14 days—*Leucorrhœa* Not examined	Debility, nervous depression, bearing down pain, piles	6 weeks	Cured. Leuchorrœa not reported	*Ign.* 3—*Ign.* 3.
143	19 Single	some years	*Menses* irregular, scanty, and pale—copious *Leucorrhœa* Not examined	*Nausea*, dyspepsia, pain in back, depression	3 months	But little benefit, left treatment too soon	*Puls.* 6—Bell. 30
144	16 Single		*Menses* irregular, very scanty Not examined	*Debility*, short breath	2 weeks	No change whilst under observation, left too soon to judge. I heard afterwards that she was better.	Tr. Sulph. O
145	38 married, 6 children. youngest 4 months.	2 months	*Menses* absent, is nursing—yellow *Leucorrhœa* Examined—ARGENTI NIT.	Pain in left mamma, pain in loins, weight in hypogastrium Inflammation and ulceration of cervix	3½ months	Uterus cured, health improved, at once became pregnant, when ulcer was healed; the pain in mamma ceased when uterus became well.	*Puls.* 3x.

146	24 Single	several years	*Menses* very irregular, often absent, are so now—occasional *Leucorrhœa* Not examined	Dyspepsia, constipation, headache	3 months	Very much benefitted, menses returned and continued regular for some months; subject, however, to relapses.	Nux v. 3—*Lyc.* 5 6 12 30 100.
147	24 Single	some time	*Menses* regular, scanty, pale—much *Leucorrhœa* Not examined	Debility, much headache, dyspepsia, pain in back	2 months	Very much relieved—menses came of a natural color; leucorrhœa continued and also pain in back; gave up treatment too soon	Sulph. 30—Merc. 12—Sulph. 30—Graph. 30.
148	19 Single	a long time	*Menses* regular—*Leucorrhœa* Not examined	*Severe pain in sacrum*, palpitation	4½ months	Much benefitted in health—*Leucorrhœa* not reported	Bell. 3—Sep. 12—Puls. 6—*Plumb.* 6—*Puls.* 6—Tr. Sulph. O.
149	22 Single	4 or 5 years	*Menses* regular, painful—much *Leucorrhœa* Not examined	*Pain in hepatic region*, dysmenorrhœa	2 months	Cured, leucorrhœa ceased	Nux v. 6 30—Sulph. 30 Merc. 6—*Sulph.* 30.
150	37 married	12 months	*Menses* regular—copious yellow *Leucorrhœa* Not examined	*Leucorrhœa*, headache, dyspepsia, weakness in loins	5½ months	Very much relieved; leucorrhœa much reduced in quantity	Lach. 12—Sep. 12—Sep. 30—*Sulph.* 30—*Calc.* 30.
151	42 married	many years	*Menses* regular, copious, with much pain—copious *Leucorrhœa* Not examined	*Pain in abdomen*, headache, much palpitation	10 months	Varied much, no essential change	Calc. 30—Ars. 12—Graph. 30—Chin. s. 1.
152	38 married	16 months	*Menses* regular—copious *Leucorrhœa* Not examined	Pain in right side of abdomen, severe headache at times	6 weeks	Not much change, left treatment too soon	Sulph. 30—Sep. 12.
153	30–5 married	a long time	*Menses* regular—slight *Leucorrhœa* Not examined	*Great debility*, hysteria; formerly had ulcerated cervix, under Dr. Simpson	6 months	Decidedly benefitted, and continued to improve under Homœopathic care; was formerly treated locally by Dr. Simpson	Tr. Sulph. O—Calc. a. 3—Alum. 30—Sulph. 30—*Bry.* 30.
154	15 Single	3 months	*Menses* suppressed—copious *Leucorrhœa* Not examined	*Backache*, severe headache	10 days	Menses returned, and she felt so well as not to desire further treatment	*Puls.* 6.

No.	Age.	Length of illness.	Uterine Discharge.	Chief symptoms.	Length of time under treatment.	Result.	Remedies which relieved.
155	18 Single	some time	*Menses* irregular Not examined	Irregular menses, headache, swelled legs During treatment she had smallpox, which was treated by Acon. 3. and Tart. em. 1.	3 months	Cured	Puls. 6.—***Ferr. ac.*** 2.
156	28 Single	some years	***Menses*** irregular, scanty, painful or not — occasional ***Leucorrhœa*** Not examined	Dysmenorrhœa, hysteria, severe pain in back, &c., ***debility***	11 months	Many symptoms relieved at times, but she continued very weak, and at last went under allopathic treatment, and still continues (4 years later) without any material change. All kinds of local treatment have been tried, I believe	Calc. 3—***Calc.*** 100—Sep. 100
157	40 Single	some years	***Menses*** are leaving her, often violent and clotted Examined 'TOUCHER'	Œdematous legs, throbbing and cutting hypogastric pain, *vertical headache* Hardness and irregularity of cervix—scirrhus?	6 months	No material improvement	Carb. v. 3—Puls. 3.
158	34 Single	4 years	*Menses* too early, scanty, and bright red—much ***Leucorrhœa*** Not examined	***Pain in back***, *leucorrhœa*, pain in hypogastrium, pimples on face	5 months	Very much benefitted; menses became more healthy, and leucorrhœa less	Nux v. 3x.—Sep. 5—Nux v. 3x.—***Sep.*** 12.
159	18 Single	12 months	***Menses*** absent 12 months —slight ***Leucorrhœa*** Not examined	Headache, flushing, pain round waist	1 month	Cured, has had frequent returns of Amenorrhœa, always, however, benefitted by treatment	Nux v. 6—***Puls.*** 6—***Bell.*** 6.

160	30 Single	several years	*Menses* every three weeks, scanty and pale, copious ***Leucorrhœa*** Examined, and treated by ARGENTI NIT. and Simpson's pessary	***Hysteria***, pain in right side, pain in back, vertical headache Retroversion, inflammation and ulceration of cervical canal	3 yrs. and 2 months, occasionally	General health improved, is still far from well	Nux v. 3—***Bell.*** 3—Bell. 30—Nux v. 12—Sep. 6—Tr. Sulph. O—Silie. 6 ***Kali c.*** 3—***Nux v.*** 3x.
161	23 married,	2 years	***Menses*** irregular, too seldom, scanty and pale—much ***Leucorrhœa*** Not examined	Palpitation, debility, pain above left hip, throbbing of carotids, 'bruit de diable,' frequent headache	5½ months	Very much benefitted	Puls. 30—***Puls.*** 30—Puls. 12—***Sep.*** 30—Sulph. 30 ***Sep.*** 30.
162	24 Single	some time	***Menses*** scanty and painful—slight ***Leucorrhœa*** Not examined	Flushing, and at times erysipelas of face, insufficient menses, swelled legs	4½ months	Much benefitted	Nux v. 6—Sulph. 12—Sulph. 12—Sep. 12—Puls. 6.
163	48 married,	12 months	***Menses*** abundant, hæmorrhagic clotted—copious ***Leucorrhœa*** Not examined	***Menorrhagia***, occipital headache, ***great debility***	4¾ months	Cured of the flooding, and greatly improved in health; after *menses* left her, an ulcer broke out in one leg, and continues to discharge	***Arsen.*** 12—***Chin.*** 6—***Arsen.*** 12—Ars. 6—Arsen. 30.
164	51 Single	2 years	***Menses*** ceased three years—yellow ***Leucorrhœa*** Not examined	***Debility***, flushing, dyspnœa, swelling of vulva at times	1 month	Greatly improved	***Bry.*** 6—***Sulph.*** 6.
165	31 married, no children	a year	***Menses*** copious and weakening—bloody ***Leucorrhœa***, copious Examined 'TOUCHER'	***Some bearing down pain*** Tenderness of anterior wall of uterus (Metritis?)	20 days	Some relief—left treatment toosoon	Nux v. 3x.—***Bry.*** 3x.
166	22 Single	a long time	***Menses*** regular—copious ***Leucorrhœa*** Not examined	***Hæmorrhoids***, dyspepsia, leucorrhœa, pain in back, (contracted syphilis during treatment)	3½ months	Cured both of original disease and syphilis	Acon. 6—Sulph. 30—Puls. 30—(Merc. 6—***Thuja*** 6—***Merc.*** 6.)

No.	Age.	Length of illness	Uterine discharge.	Chief symptoms.	Length of time under treatment.	Result.	Remedies which relieved.
167	38 married,	3 years	*Menses* too frequent, copious and clotted—dirty white *Leucorrhœa*, copious	*Menorrhagia*, *leucorrhœa*, headache, dyspepsia	10½ months	No permanent benefit; was dismissed because she refused to be examined	Cham. 6—Sep. 12—Lach. 30—Secale 30—Puls. 30.
			Not examined				
168	25 married,	3 years	*Menses* regular, painful—much thick *Leucorrhœa*	Gastrodynia, enuresis, headache, pain in left side	4 months not regularly	Much improvement, *leucorrhœa* lessened; not much change in enuresis	Bell. 30 — Arsen. 30 — Calc. 12.
			Not examined				
169	41 married 5 children, youngest 7	6 or 8 months	*Menses* regular and painful—copious yellow *Leucorrhœa*,	*Leucorrhœa*, debility, depression, violent headache, pain in back	1 year and 7 months	No permanent improvement before or after local treatment, which was commenced after 1 year and 4 months	Sep. 5 — Bell. 3 — *Calc. acet.* 3—*Sep.* 5—Puls. 12—Ignat. 3—*Sep.* 5.
			Examined and treated by ARGENTI NIT., KALI BICHR., AURUM. MUR., PLAT. CHL.	Ulceration of cervical canal and cervix			
170	31 married, 4 children, youngest 2	2 years	*Menses* regular, scanty, very dark—copious *Leucorrhœa*	Headache, dyspepsia, *leucorrhœa*, some cough	6½ months	Cured	Puls. 30—Calc. 30—Puls. 6—Sulph. 30—Calc. 30 Sep. 12—Calc. 30.
			Not examined				
171	30 Single	1 year	*Menses* absent 3 months—copious yellow *Leucorrhœa*	Debility, *yellow leucorrhœa*, bearing down	3 weeks	Improving, still under treatment	Sep. 3x.
			Examined, treated locally —ARGENTI NIT.	Large unhealthy ulcer of cervix			
172	27 married, a widow, 3 children	8 years	*Menses* regular—copious purulent *Leucorrhœa*	Cough, violent retching, debility, bearing down	3 weeks	Improving, still under treatment	Bell. 3x.—Arg. 3x.
			Examined, treated locally —ARGENTI NIT.	Large unhealthy ulcer of cervix			

173	37 married, a widow, 1 child	3 years	*Menses* too seldom, but very copious and debilitating Examined and treated locally at first, ARGENTI NIT.	Debility, menorrhagia, bearing down, swelled legs Cervix enlarged, finely granular, bleeding easily	3 months	Improving, still under treatment	Plat. Chl. 3—***Plat.* 12**—(locally ARGENTI NIT. once and PLAT. CHLOR. once cured the cervix completely)
174	39 married, 1 child	9 months	*Menses* absent — copious *Leucorrhœa* Examined, treated locally, ARGENTI NIT., AURUM M.	Dyspepsia, with redness and rawness of mouth, prolapsus uteri Cervix uteri projects externally, and is cleft in two, and the interior of lips are granulated.	4 months	Cured. General treatment relieved the general health, but uterus remained unchanged till local treatment commenced; the prolapse and ulceration were both completely cured	Bell. 3x.—***Bell.* 1**—***Nux v.* 3x.**—***Aurum Mur.* 1-50**, locally and internally ***Aur. Mur.* 3.**
175	40 married, 2 children, youngest 11	2 years	*Menses* regular Examined, treated locally, ARGENTI NIT. and KALI BICHROM.	*Headache*, pain and occasional hæmorrhage after coition Smooth induration of anterior lip, canal red and raw	3 months	Greatly improved, left treatment too soon; anterior lip smaller, and canal more healthy	Puls. 3—Ign. 3x.—***K. Bich.* 3x.**
176	35 married, a widow, 2 children, youngest 6	12 months	*Menses* regular, scanty—copious *Leucorrhœa* Examined and treated locally, ARGENTI NIT. and KALI BICHROM.	*Bearing down pain*, pain in groins Retroflexion of cervix, soft enlargement of cervix, os and canal patent and excoriated	5 months	Cured; is still dyspeptic, and has inguinal hernia	Nux v. 12—Bell. 3x.—Aur. M. 3—Nux v. 3—Sulph. 3—K. Bich. 3x.
177	35 married, a widow, 3 children, youngest 11	8 or 9 years	*Menses* much too copious—copious *Leucorrhœa* Not examined	*Menorrhagia*, debility, backache	3 months	Greatly benefitted, still under treatment	Bell. 3x.—Plat. Chl. 3.
178	29 married, twins four and a half years ago	5 years	*Menses* regular — thick white *Leucorrhœa*, copious Examined, treated locally, AURUM MUR. and STANNUM CHLOR.	Prolapsus uteri Labiæ uteri greatly enlarged, and projecting from vagina	5 weeks	Decidedly benefitted, uterus entirely within vagina; left treatment too soon	Aur. M. 3—Stann. 3x.—(Puls. 3x.)

No.	Age.	Length of illness.	Uterine discharge.	Chief symptoms.	Length of time under treatment.	Results.	Remedies which relieved.
179	30—5 married, 1 child, 20 months old	20 months	*Menses* absent (is pregnant)—*Leucorrhœa* Examined 'TOUCHER' once	Debility, *leucorrhœa*, shooting pains in vagina Reported by a London physician to have vaginitis and ulcerated cervix	5 months occasionally	Much benefitted; was delivered of a healthy child one month after, but some of the uterine symptoms returned afterwards	Nux v. 3.—Car. v. 5.
180	40 married, 8 or 9 children, youngest 2 years and a half	6 or 8 months	*Menses* very copious—some *Leucorrhœa* Examined, treated locally, ARGENTI NIT.	Debility, Menorrhagia, bearing down Enlargement, and granulated excoriation of cervix	4 months	Decidedly better; after the second application of ARGENTI NIT. there came an induration of anterior lip exactly resembling that occurring in chronic inflammation	Plat. 6—Arg. 3x.

TABLE No. 1.

GENERAL TABLE.

No. of Cases cured or greatly benefitted	112	
No. of Cases somewhat benefitted	51	
No. of Cases unchanged	17	
		180
No. of Cases still under treatment	22	
No. of Cases left treatment to early to judge	34	

TABLE No. 2, Showing Ages and Results.

State.	Ages.	Cured or greatly benefitted.	Somewhat benefitted	Unchanged.	Still under treatment	Total.		Left treatment too early to judge. State.	Ages.	Cured or greatly benefitted.	Somewhat benefitted.	Unchanged.	Total.	
Married..	15—20	..	..	..	..	..	33	Married..	15—20	..	..	..	..	7
Single...	..	18	14	2	..	33		Single...	..	3	4	..	7	
Married..	20—25	7	2	..	..	9	46	Married..	20—25	2	..	..	2	11
Single...	..	26	8	2	..	37		Single...	..	7	1	1	9	
Married..	25—30	5	5	1	..	11	27	Married..	25—30	1	4	..	5	6
Single...	..	7	4	5	..	16		Single...	..	1	..	..	1	
Married..	30—35	14	5	1	..	20	33	Married..	30—35	2	1	..	3	3
Single...	..	10	2	1	..	13		Single...	..	..	..	..	..	
Married..	35—40	15	4	2	..	21	25	Married..	35—40	1	1	2	4	4
Single...	..	2	2	..	..	4		Single...	..	..	..	..	..	
Married..	40—50	5	4	3	..	12	16	Married..	40—50	1	1	..	2	3
"	50 and upwds.	2	1	..	..	3		"	50 and upwds.	..	..	1	1	
Single...	..	1	..	..	..	1		Single...	..	..	..	..	..	..
Married and families		34	13	3	..	51	51	Married and families		7	3	1	..	11
							180							

TABLE No. 3, Showing Length of Illness and Results.

Time.	Cured or greatly benefitted.	Somewhat benefitted	Unchanged.	Still under treatment	Total.	Left treatment too early to judge. Time.	Cured or greatly benefitted.	Somewhat benefitted.	Unchanged.	Still under treatment.	Total.
Under 3 months	14	5	..	1	19	Under 3 months	1	1	..	..	2
.. 6 ..	9	4	..	3	13	.. 6 ..	1	1	..	..	2
.. 12 ..	16	9	2	3	27	.. 12 ..	3	1	1	..	5
.. 2 years..	14	4	3	3	21	.. 2 years..	2	3	2	..	7
.. 3 ..	9	5	1	2	16	.. 3 ..	3	1	..	..	4
.. 6 ..	10	3	1	1	13	.. 6 ..	4	..	..	..	4
Many years.....	18	17	8	8	43	Many years....	..	2	1	..	3
A long time....	20	3	2	1	25	A long time....	4	1	..	..	5
Unknown	2	1	..	..	3	Unknown	1	1	..	..	2
					180						

TABLE No. 4, Showing Length of Time under Treatment.

Time.	Cases under treatment steadily.					Cases seen occasionally.					Cases left too early to judge.			
	Cured or greatly benefitted.	Somewhat benefitted	Unchanged.	Still under treatment	Total.	Cured or greatly benefitted.	Somewhat benefitted	Unchanged.	Total.	Correct Total.	Cured or greatly benefitted.	Somewhat benefitted	Unchanged.	Total
1 month and under.....	12	7	1	..	20	..	..	..	..	20	5	3	1	9
2	16	10	1	..	27	..	..	..	..	27	7	3	2	12
3	19	8	2	..	29	..	..	..	..	29	2	4	..	6
4	12	4	2	..	18	..	..	..	..	18	3	..	..	3
5	14	1	..	..	15	..	..	..	..	15	..	..	..	..
6	8	5	5	..	18	2	..	..	2	20	2	1	..	3
9	9	2	1	..	12	1	1	..	2	14	..	..	1	1
12	5	4	3	..	12	..	..	..	..	12	..	..	..	..
1¼ years.....	3	2	1	..	6	..	..	..	..	6	..	..	..	..
1½	2	..	..	..	2	..	1	..	1	3	..	..	..	..
2 or more yrs.	5	3	..	..	8	3	2	..	5	13	..	..	..	..
Unknown...	..	..	..	..	..	1	1	1	3	3	..	..	..	..

TABLE No. 5, Showing State of Uterine Functions.

State of Uterine functions.	Cured or greatly benefitted.	Somewhat benefitted.	Unchanged.	total.	Left treatment too early to judge.				Still under treatment.			
					Cured or greatly benefitted.	Somewhat benefitted.	Unchanged.	Total.	Greatly benefitted	Some benefit.	Unchanged.	Total.
Menses absent..	24	12	..	36	4	3	..	7	3	2	..	5
.. regular..	34	13	5	52	5	1	2	8	2	..	..	7
.. irregular.	10	4	4	18	..	2	..	2	..	5	..	..
.. scanty ..	22	8	5	35	6	1	..	7	3	1	..	4
.. copious..	23	13	6	43	2	2	1	5	5	3	..	8
.. too long duration	4	3	..	7	..	1	..	1	..	..	..	..
.. painful..	13	7	5	25	3	1	..	4	2	3	..	5
.. pale.....	12	6	1	19	4	1	1	6	..	..	..	..
.. dark....	4	3	1	8	..	1	..	1	..	..	..	..
.. too early.	10	11	1	22	3	2	..	5	4	..	..	4
.. too late..	5	2	2	9	4	..	..	4	..	2	..	2
Leuc. some...	26	6	5	37	5	3	..	8	2	2	..	4
.. copious..	50	14	9	73	9	4	3	16	4	6	..	10
.. occasional	14	8	2	24	1	2	..	3	3	1	..	4
Sang. discharge	..	..	1	1	..	..	1	1				

TABLE No. 6 SHOWING NO. OF CASES UNEXAMINED, EXAMINED, AND EXAMINED AND TREATED LOCALLY, WITH RESULTS.

Whether examined or otherwise.	Cured or greatly benefitted.	Somewhat benefitted.	Unchanged.	Total.	Left treatment too early to judge. Cured or greatly benefitted.	Somewhat benefitted.	Unchanged.	Total
Not examined	70	32	8	110	14	9	3	23
Examined	7	9	7	23	..	4	1	5
Examined and treated locally	35	10	2	47	5	1	..	6

TABLE No. 7, ANALYSIS OF CASES EXAMINED, SHOWING UTERINE SYMPTOMS, MODE OF TREATMENT AND RESULTS.

Objective Uterine symptoms.	Cured or greatly benefitted.			Somewhat benefitted.			Unchanged.			Cured.	Total.	Still under treatment.		
	Locally.	Not locally.	Mechanically.	Locally.	Not locally.	Mechanically.	Locally.	Not locally.	Mechanically.	Locally and Mechanically.		Locally.	Not locally.	Mechanically.
First stage of cervico-metritis	3	..	..	1	..	..	..	..	..	..	4	2	..	..
Second	4	1	..	1	1	..	..	..	1	..	8	1	..	..
Third	9	..	..	4	..	..	..	..	..	2	15	6	..	..
Fourth	8	1	..	..	..	..	..	..	..	..	9	1	..	..
Uterus sensitive to touch	..	1	..	..	4	..	..	2	..	..	7	..	1	..
.. engorged	..	4	5	..	3	1	..	..	..	..	13	..	1	..
.. .. posterior wall	..	..	..	..	1	..	..	..	..	2	3	..	..	..
.. .. anterior wall	..	1	..	..	1	..	..	..	..	..	2	..	..	..
Symptoms of cervico-metritis detected by the finger, where there was an opportunity of using the speculum	..	5	3	..	6	1	..	5	..	..	20	..	1	..
Anteversion of uterus	1	..	1	..	..	..	..	..	..	..	2	..	..	..
Retroversion ..	..	..	3	..	..	2	..	..	1	3	9	..	..	..
Prolapse ..	1	..	..	1	1	..	..	..	..	..	3	..	..	..
Syphilitic ulceration	..	..	..	..	1	..	..	..	..	..	1	..	..	..
Induration of posterior wall, Schirrus, qy.?	..	..	..	..	..	..	..	2	..	..	2	..	..	..
Cancer of uterus	died.	..	..	..	..	..	..	..	..	..	1	..	..	..

TABLE No. 7, Continued.

Objective Uterine symptoms.	Left treatment too early to judge. — Cured or greatly benefitted. — Locally.	Somewhat benefitted. — Locally.	Somewhat benefitted. — Not locally.	Unchanged. — Not locally.	Total.	STILL UNDER TREATMENT. — Greatly benefitted. — Locally.	Greatly benefitted. — Not locally.	Greatly benefitted. — Mechanically.	Somewhat benefitted. — Locally.	Somewhat benefitted. — Not locally.	Somewhat benefitted. — Mechanically.	Total.
First stage of cervico-metritis.	..	..	..	..	..	1	..	..	1	..	..	2
Second	..	..	1	..	1	..	..	..	1	..	..	1
Third	1	1	..	..	2	2	..	..	4	..	..	6
Fourth	1	..	..	..	1	1	..	..	..	..	..	1
Uterus sensitive to touch	..	..	3	1	4	..	1	..	..	..	..	1
.. engorged	..	..	1	..	1	..	..	..	..	1	..	1
.. .. anterior wall..	..	..	1	..	1	..	..	..	..	..	..	..
Symptoms of cervico-metritis detected by the finger, where there was no opportunity of using the speculum	..	..	1	1	4	..	..	..	..	1	..	1
Prolapse of uterus	..	..	..	..	1	..	..	..	..	..	..	..

TABLE No. 8. MEDICINES AND POTENCIES THAT DID GOOD.

Medicine			
Aconite	3	6	.
Alumina......................	3	12	30
„ 3 altern. with Bryonia...	3	.	.
„ 30 „ „ ...	30	.	.
Ammonium carbonicum.........	3x	3	5
Argentum	3x	.	.
Arsenicum	2	3	6
„	12	30	.
„ 12 altern. with China..	6	.	.
„ 12 „ Puls. ..	12	.	.
„ 30 „ „ ..	30	.	.
„ 30 „ Sulph ..	30	.	.
„ 30 „ Carb. veg.	30	.	.
Aurum	30	.	.
„ 30 altern. with Sepia......	30	.	.
Aurum muriaticum	3	.	.
Baryta carbon.	6	.	.
Belladonna....................	1	3x	2
„	3	6	12
„	18	30	.
„ 6 altern. with Sepia...	12	.	.
„ 6 „ Graph...	6	.	.
„ 6 „ Plat.....	6	.	.
„ 6 „ Puls.....	6	.	.
„ 18 „ „	6	.	.
Berberis vulg.	3	.	.
Bryonia alba	1-20	1	3x
„	3	6	12
„	30	.	.
„ 3 altern. with Alum.	3	.	.
„ 30 „ „	30	.	.
Calcarea acet..................	3	.	.
„ carbon.	3	6	12
„ „	18	30	100
„ „ 12 alt. with Zinc.	6	.	.
Cantharis	3	.	.
Carbo vegetabilis..............	3	5	6
„	12	30	.
„ 12 alt. with Cham.	6	.	.
„ 12 alt. with Lach..	12	.	.
„ 30 alt. with Arsen.	30	.	.
Chamomilla	3x	3	6
„	12	.	.
„ 6 alt. with Carb. veg.	12	.	.
China off......................	O	1	3
„	6	30	.
„ 6 altern. with Arsen....	12	.	.
Chininum sulph.	1	.	.
Cina	3x	.	.
Cocculus	3	6	.
Conium	1	3	.
Digitalis	3	6	.
Ferrum	6	12	.
„ acet.	2	.	.
„ sulph.	1x	.	.
Graphites	3	5	6
„	12	30	.
„ 6 altern. with Bell.	6	.	.
„ 6 „ Sepia	12	.	.
Hypericum......................	3x	.	.
Ignatia	3x	3	6
Iodium	2	.	.

TABLE No. 8.—Continued.

Remedy			
Kali Bichrom	3x	2	6
„ carbon.	3x	3	6
„ „	12	.	.
„ Iodidum	1	.	.
Kali Iodid. 1 alt. with Merc. acet.	1	.	.
Kreosotum	3x	2	12
„ 12 altern. with Puls.	12	.	.
Lachesis	6	12	30
" 12 altern. with Carb. veg.	12	.	.
„ 12 „ Sepia	12	.	.
Lycopodium	5	12	30
Magnesia carb.	6	.	.
Manganum acet.	1	.	.
Mercurius acet.	1	3x	.
„ 1 alt. with Kali Iod.	1	.	.
„ iodid.	1	3x	.
„ sol.	3	5	6
„ „	12	.	.
„ Subl. Corr.	2	.	.
Natrum muriat.	3	6	12
Nitri. acidum	2	.	.
Nux moschata	3x	6	.
„ vomica	3x	3	6
„ „	12	30	.
Phosphorus	3	30	.
Platina	3	6	12
„ 6 altern. with Puls.	6	.	.
„ 6 „ Bell.	6	.	.
Platinum Chlor	3	.	.
Plumbum	6	12	.
„ acet.	1	.	.
Pulsatilla	1	3x	3
„	6	12	30
„ 3 altern. with Sulph.	6	.	.
„ 6 „ Plat.	6	.	.
Pulsatilla 6 „ Sulph.	12	.	.
„ 6 „ „	6	.	.
„ 6 „ Sepia	12	.	.
„ 6 „ Bell.	18	.	.
„ 6 „ Sepia	6	.	.
„ 6 „ Bell.	6	.	.
„ 12 „ Arsen.	12	.	.
„ 12 „ Kreos.	12	.	.
„ 30 „ Arsen.	30	.	.
Rhus Tox	3x	6	.
Sabina	3x	6	.
Secale Corn	3	6	30
Sepia	3x	3	5
„	6	12	30
„	100	.	.
„ 6 altern. with Puls.	6	.	.
„ 12 „ „	6	.	.
„ 12 „ Bell.	6	.	.
„ 12 „ Graph.	6	.	.
„ 12 „ Sulph.	12	.	.
„ 12 „ Lach.	12	.	.
„ 30 „ Aurum	30	.	.
Silicea	6	.	.
Stannum	3x	.	.
Sulphur	3	6	12
„	30	.	.
„ 6 altern. with Puls.	6	.	.
„ 6 „ Puls.	3	.	.
„ 12 „ Sepia	12	.	.
„ 30 „ Arsen	30	.	.
Sulphuris tinct.	O	.	.
Thuja Occ.	3	.	.
Vinca	1-20	1	.
Zincum	6	.	.
„ 6 altern. with Calcar.	12	.	.

TABLE No. 9, SHOWING REMEDIES MOST FREQUENTLY USEFUL FOR CHIEF SYMPTOMS.

Symptoms.	Total Number reported	Remedy and potency most frequently useful.	Number reported.	Number relieved by various potencies.	Ditto in alternation with other remedies	Total.
1. *Debility*	95	1 Pulsatilla 3	12	39	5	44
		2 Sepia 30	11	27	3	30
2. *Headache*	51	1 Pulsatilla . . . 3	10	30	5	35
		 6	10			
		2 Sepia	..	13	2	15
		3 Nux vomica .	..	12	..	12
3. *Pain in back*	50	1 Sepia 12	8	26	3	29
		 30	8			
		3 Sulphur 30	8	18	3	21
		2 Pulsatilla	..	19	5	24
		4 Belladonna . .	..	16	1	17
		5 Nux vomica . .	..	15	..	15
4. *Neuralgiæ*	31	1 Pulsatilla 6 12 30	5	15	1	16
		2 Tr. Sulphur . . O	5	11	1	12
		3 Nux vomica .	..	12	..	12
5. *Leucorrhœa*	29	2 Sulphur 30	9	14	..	14
		1 Sepia	..	15	2	17
		3 Pulsatilla . . .	..	8	..	8
6. *Dyspepsia*	27	1 Pulsatilla, 6 12 30	7	18	..	18
		2 Belladonna . .	..	10	..	10
		3 Nux vomica .	..	10	..	10
7. *Bearing down pain*	24	1 Nux vomica . 3x	3	9	..	9
		2 Pulsatilla 12	3	8	..	8
		3 Sepia 30	3	6	..	6
		4 Bryonia 3x	3	4	..	4
		5 Ignatia 3	3	3	..	3

TABLE No. 9.—Continued.

	Symptoms.	Total Number reported.	Remedy and Potency most frequently useful.		Number reported.	Number relieved by various potencies	Ditto in alternation with other remedies.	Total.
8.	*Pain in left side*	18	Pulsatilla	3	7	10	..	10
9.	*Pains in abdomen* ...	16	1 Tr. Sulphur .	O	4	7	..	7
			2 Pulsatilla		..	7	..	7
10.	*Menorrhagia*	15	1 Platin. Chlor .	3	3	3 } 11	..	11
			Platina		..	8 }		
			2 Belladonna ..	3x	3	5	4	9
			3 Sulphur	30	3	..	..	3
11.	*Dysmenorrhœa*	14	1 Pulsatilla	6	4	5	3	8
			2 Sepia	12	4	7	1	8
12.	*Pain in hypogastrium.*	14	1 Nux vomica .	3	4	8	..	8
			2 Lachesis	6	4	4	..	4
13.	*Cardiac symptoms* ...	12	1 Pulsatilla	3	5	13	2	15
			3 Sepia	30	5	7	..	7
			2 Sulphur		..	8	..	8
14.	*Amenorrhœa*	11	1 Pulsatilla	3	3	6	3	9
			2 Sulphur		..	5	..	5
15.	*Constipation*	10	Nux vomica .	3	3	6	..	6
			Pulsatilla	3	3	6	..	6
16.	*Anæmia and Chlorosis*	9	1 Pulsatilla	3	2 }	7	2	9
			....	6	2 }			
			....	30	2 }			
			2 Belladonna ..	6	2	3	4	7
			3 Sepia	30	2	2	3	5
			4 Platina	6	2	1	2	3
17.	*Shortness of breath* ..	7	3 Sepia	5	3	4	..	4
			1 Pulsatilla		..	6	..	6
			2 Sulphur		..	6	..	6
			4 Belladonna ..		..	3	..	3
			5 Nux vomica .		..	3	..	3
18.	*Swelled legs*	6	Pulsatilla	3	2 }	5	2	7
			....	6	2 }			

1	*Pulsatilla* occurs among the most useful in	16	symptoms, as chief in	12
2	*Sepia* ,, ,,	9	,, ,,	2
3	*Nux vomica* ,, ,,	8	,, ,,	3
4	*Sulphur* ,, ,,	8	,, ,,	1

TABLE No. 10, Showing Relative Results of High and Low Potencies.

N.B.—The low potencies include 6 and under—The high potencies, 12 and above.	Low potencies exclusively.	High potencies exclusively.	Total.	Left treatment too early. Low potencies exclusively.	Left treatment too early. High potencies exclusively.	Left treatment too early. Total.
Cured or greatly benefitted	62	16	78	5	5	10
Somewhat benefitted ...	23	7	30	5	1	6
Unchanged	7	7	10	1	1	2

Results of Treatment with both High and Low Potencies.

Cases in which both high and low potencies were given with decidedly more benefit from the low than the high	19
Cases in which no marked difference was observable between the effects of high and low potencies	46

TABLE No. 11, SHOWING FREQUENCY OF OCCURRENCE OF VARIOUS SYMPTOMS AS A CHIEF SOURCE OF COMPLAINT.

SYMPTOMS.	Cured or greatly benefitted.	Somewhat benefitted.	Unchanged.	Still under treatment.	Left treatment too early to judge.	Total.	SYMPTOMS.	Cured or greatly benefitted.	Somewhat benefitted.	Unchanged.	Still under treatment.	Left treatment too early to judge.	Total.
1 Debility	54	29	12	17	17	95	30 Eruptions on the skin	3	..	..	..	..	3
2 Headache	28	16	7	6	7	51	31 Nervousness	..	1	1	2	..	2
3 Pain in back	28	18	4	10	10	50	32 Epileptic fits	1	1	..	..	1	2
4 Neuralgiæ	16	9	6	..	4	31	33 Irregular menses	1	1	..	..	..	2
5 Leucorrhœa	19	9	1	2	5	29	34 Cough	1	1	..	1	..	2
6 Dyspepsia	22	5	..	2	7	27	35 Numbness of right arm and leg	2	..	..	..	..	2
7 Bearing down pain	14	8	2	5	5	24	36 Pain in the thighs	1	1	..	..	1	2
8 Pain in left side	13	3	2	..	7	18	37 Pelvic abscess	..	2	..	..	..	2
9 Pains in abdomen	9	6	1	2	..	16	38 Throbbing of carotids	1	..	1	..	..	2
10 Menorrhagia	10	4	1	3	3	15	39 Hæmorrhoids	2	..	..	..	..	2
11 Dysmenorrhœa	6	3	5	1	1	14	40 Palpitation	..	1	..	1	..	1
12 Pain in hypogastrium	9	3	2	1	1	14	41 Pain in right ovary	..	..	1	1	..	1
13 Cardiac symptoms	7	3	2	1	3	12	42 Vertigo	1	..	..	..	..	1
14 Amenorrhœa	6	4	1	..	..	11	43 Congestion of head	1	..	..	..	..	1
15 Constipation	5	3	2	..	1	10	44 Irregular action of heart	..	..	1	..	..	1
16 Anœmia and Chlorosis	2	5	2	2	2	9	45 Spinal irritation	..	1	..	..	..	1
17 Shortness of breath	3	3	1	2	2	7	46 Hepatic pain	1	..	..	..	..	1
18 Swelled legs	5	..	1	1	..	6	47 Hysterical convulsions	..	..	1	..	..	1
19 Pains in various parts	1	2	2	1	..	5	48 Sanguineous discharge	..	..	1	..	1	1
20 Pain in left ovary	2	3	..	..	1	5	49 Hæmorrhage from rectum	1	..	..	..	..	1
21 Nausea	3	1	1	..	1	5	50 Discharge of pus per anum	1	..	..	..	..	1
22 Pain in right side	3	1	1	1	1	5	51 Great distension of abdomen	1	..	..	..	..	1
23 Vomiting	2	2	..	3	..	4	52 Pain in genitals	1	..	..	..	..	1
24 Flushed face	4	..	..	..	..	4	53 Apthæ in mouth	..	1	..	..	..	1
25 Fainting fits	2	2	..	..	..	4	54 Varicose veins	1	..	..	..	..	1
26 Sinking in stomach	3	1	..	1	1	4	55 Swelled glands	1	..	..	..	..	1
27 Pain in iliac region	2	1	..	1	..	3	56 Pain in left mamma	1	..	..	..	..	1
28 Irritable bladder	2	1	..	1	..	3	57 Pain & hæmorrhoids after coitus	1	..	..	..	1	1
29 Pain in hypochondria	2	1	..	..	1	3	58 Shooting pains in vagina	1	..	..	..	..	1

TABLE No. 12, Showing Local Remedies with Results.

Local remedies employed.	Cured or greatly benefitted.	Somewhat benefitted.	Unchanged.	Did harm.	Total.
Nitrate of Silver	22	7	..	..	29
Bichromate of Potash	1	3	..	..	4
Potassa Fusa............	1	1	..	..	2
Pernitrate of Mercury....	2	1	..	..	3
Simpson's pessary........	6	1	..	2	9
Scofield's pessary........	1	..	..	..	1
Douche................	8	1	4	..	13
Uterine sound..........	2	..	..	..	2
Aurum muriaticum, 1 50.	2	..	..	..	2
Stannum muriaticum.....	1	..	..	..	1

TABLE No. 13, Showing Social Condition of those Examined, Examined and Treated Locally, and also Locally and Mechanically.

Whether examined or otherwise.	Married	Single.	Total.	
Examined..................	13	10	23	
Examined and treated locally....	28	8	36	47
Examined and treated locally and mechanically..........	1	5	6	
Examined and treated mechanically....................	4	1	5	

TABLE No. 14, Showing the Ages of those examined, treated locally, &c.

State.	Age.	Cured or greatly benefitted.				Somewhat benefitted.				Unchanged.				Total.	
		Locally.	Not Locally.	Mechanically.	Locally and Mechanically.	Locally.	Not locally.	Mechanically.	Locally and Mechanically.	Locally.	Not Locally.	Mechanically	Locallly and Mechanically.		
Single....	Under 15	..	1	..	..	..	..	..	..	..	..	..	..		1
.. ....	15—20	1	..	..	..	..	3	..	..	..	..	..	..		4
Married...	20—25	1	2	..	..	..	..	..	..	..	..	..	..	3	9
Single....	..—..	1	..	..	2	2	..	..	..	..	1	..	..	6	
Married...	25—30	4	..	1	1	2	..	..	..	..	1	1	..	10	13
Single....	..—..	1	..	1	..	..	..	..	..	..	1	..	..	3	
Married...	30—35	4	2	1	..	2	3	..	..	..	4	..	..	16	26
Single....	..—..	2	1	..	2	1	3	..	1	..	..	..	..	10	
Married...	35—40	10	..	1	..	2	..	..	..	..	..	..	..		13
.. ....	40—50	1	1	..	..	..	..	..	..	1	..	..	..		3
.. ....	50 and upwards.	1	..	..	..	..	..	..	..	..	..	..	..		1

TABLE No. 2, Continued. STILL UNDER TREATMENT.

State.	Age.	Greatly benefitted.	Somewhat benefitted.	Unchanged.	Total.	
Single	15—20	1	2	..	3	
.. ....	20—25	1	4	..	5	
Married ..	25—30	..	1	..	1	} 3
Single	..—..	1	1	..	2	
Married ..	30—35	1	1	..	2	} 6
Single	..—..	2	2	..	4	
Married ..	30—40	4	..	..	4	
.. ....	40—50	..	1	..	1	
Married and families ..		5	2	..	7	

TABLE No. 3, Continued. STILL UNDER TREATMENT.

Length of illness.	Greatly benefitted.	Somewhat benefitted.	Unchanged.	Total.
Under 3 months	..	1	..	1
.. 6 ..	1	2	..	3
.. 12 ..	1	2	..	3
.. 2 years..	3	..	..	3
.. 3 ..	2	..	..	2
.. 6 ..	1	..	..	1
Many years....	2	5	1	8
A long time....	..	1	..	1

TABLE No. 4, Continued. STILL UNDER TREATMENT.

Length of treatment.	Greatly benefitted.	Somewhat benefitted.	Unchanged.	Total.
Under 1 month	..	3	..	3
.. 2 ..	..	1	..	1
.. 3 ..	3	1	..	4
.. 4 ..	1	..	..	1
.. 5 ..	2	..	..	2
.. 6 ..	..	1	..	1
.. 9 ..	2	1	..	3
.. 12 ..	1	..	..	1
.. 1¼ years	1	..	..	1
.. 1½ ..	..	1	..	1
2 or more years	3	1	..	4

TABLE No. 6, Continued. STILL UNDER TREATMENT.

Whether examined or otherwise.	Greatly benefitted.	Some benefit.	Unchanged.	Total.
Not examined	5	3	..	8
Examined	1	1	..	2
Examined and treated locally	6	6	..	12

TABLE No. 15, being Analysis of Cases of Leucorrhœa, Section 1.

State.	Ages.												Still under treatment.										Left treatment too early.									
		Cured or greatly bene-fitted.			Some-what bene-fitted.			Un-changed.					Great-ly bene-fitted.			Some-what bene-fitted.			Un-changed.				Cured or greatly bene-fitted.			Some-what bene-fitted.			Un-changed.			
		Some leucorrhœa.	Cop. leucorrhœa.	Ocsnl. leucorrhœa.	Some leucorrhœa.	Cop. leucorrhœa.	Ocsnl. leucorrhœa.	Some leucorrhœa.	Cop. leucorrhœa.	Ocsnl. leucorrhœa.	Total.		Some leucorrhœa	Cop. leucorrhœa.	Ocsnl. leucorrhœa.	Some leucorrhœa.	Cop. leucorrhœa.	Ocsnl. leucorrhœa.	Some leucorrhœa.	Cop. leucorrhœa.	Ocsnl. leucorrhœa.	Total.	Some leucorrhœa.	Cop. leucorrhœa.	Ocsnl. leucorrhœa.	Some leucorrhœa.	Cop leucorrhœa.	Ocsnl leucorrhœa.	Some leucorrhœa.	Cop. leucorrhœa.	Ocsnl. leucorrhœa.	Total.
Single ..	Under 15	..	1	..	..	..	..	..	..	..	..	1	..	..	..	..	..	..	..	..	..	..	..	..	..	..	..	..	..	..	..	..
— ..	15—20	4	5	..	1	..	2	..	2	..	..	14	..	..	..	..	1	1	..	..	..	2	2	1	..	1	1	..	..	..	..	5
Married .	20—25	1	5	1	..	..	..	..	..	..	7	17	..	..	..	..	..	..	..	..	..	..	1	1	..	..	..	1	..	..	..	3
Single ..	..—..	2	4	2	..	2	..	..	..	..	10		..	1	..	..	1	..	..	..	..	2	..	5	1	1	..	..	..	1	..	8
Married .	25—30	..	4	1	..	..	..	1	..	1	7	14	..	1	..	..	1	..	..	..	..	2	..	2	..	..	1	1	..	..	..	4
Single ..	..—..	2	1	..	1	..	..	2	..	1	7		..	..	1	..	2	1	..	..	..	4	..	..	..	..	..	..	..	..	..	..
Married .	30—35	2	5	..	..	..	..	1	1	..	9	20	1	1	..	..	..	..	..	..	..	2	1	..	..	..	1	..	..	..	..	2
Single ..	..—..	4	1	2	..	2	2	..	..	..	11		..	..	2	1	..	..	..	..	..	3	..	..	..	..	..	..	..	..	..	..
Married .	35—40	..	8	1	..	..	..	1	2	..	12	13	2	..	..	..	..	..	..	..	..	2	1	..	..	..	..	..	..	1	..	2
Single ..	..—..	..	..	1	..	..	..	..	..	..	1		..	..	..	..	..	..	..	..	..	..	..	..	..	..	..	..	..	..	..	..
Married .	40—50	2	2	2	..	..	..	..	1	..	..	7	..	..	..	..	..	1	..	..	..	1	1	..	..	..	1	..	..	..	..	2
Married .	50 and upwards.	..	1	1	..	..	..	..	..	..	2		..	..	..	..	..	..	..	..	..	..	..	..	..	..	..	..	..	1	..	1
Single ..	..—..	..	1	..	..	..	..	..	..	..	1		..	..	..	..	..	..	..	..	..	..	..	..	..	..	..	..	..	..	..	..
With families ..		3	13	4	..	1	..	2	1	..	24	24	3	2	..	..	2	..	..	..	..	7	3	3	..	..	1	2	..	..	..	9

TABLE No. 16, being Analysis of cases of Leucorrhœa, Section 2.

Comparative Numbers of Examined, Unexamined, &c.											Still under treatment.										Left treatment too early to judge									
	Cured or greatly benefit'd.			Some-what benefit'd.			Un-changed.				Greatly benefit'd.			Some-what benefit'd.			Un-changed.				Cured or greatly benefit'd.			Some what benefit'd.			Un-changed.			
	Some Leucorrhœa.	Cop. Leucorrhœa.	Ocsnl. Leucorrhœa.	Some Leucorrhœa.	Cop. Leucorrhœa.	Ocsnl. Leucorrhœa.	Some Leucorrhœa.	Cop. Leucorrhœa.	Ocsnl. Leucorrhœa.	Total.	Some Leucorrhœa.	Cop. Leucorrhœa.	Ocsnl. Leucorrhœa.	Sbme Leucorrhœa.	Cop. Leucorrhœa.	Ocsnl. Leucorrhœa.	Some Leucorrhœa.	Cop. Leucorrhœa.	Ocsnl. Leucorrhœa.	Total.	Some Leucorrhœa.	Cop. Leucorrhœa.	Ocsnl. Leucorrhœa.	Some Leucorrhœa.	Cop. Leucorrhœa.	Ocsnl. Leucorrhœa.	Some Leucorrhœa.	Cop. Leucorrhœa.	Ocsnl. Leucorrhœa.	Total.
Not examined	13	24	4	2	3	2	3	5	1	57	..	1	1	1	1	1	..	..	..	5	3	7	1	1	2	1	..	3	..	18
Examined	1	3	1	..	1	2	2	..	..	10	1	..	..	..	1	..	..	..	..	2	..	..	..	1	2	1	..	..	..	4
Examined and treated locally..	2	7	4	..	..	..	..	1	..	14	2	2	1	..	3	1	..	..	..	9	2	2	..	..	..	..	..	..	..	4
Do. .. do. mechanically	..	2	1	..	..	1	..	..	1	4	..	..	..	..	..	..	..	..	..	..	..	..	..	1	..	..	..	..	..	1
Do. .. do. locally and mechanically	2	1	1	..	..	..	..	..	..	4	..	1	..	..	1	..	..	..	..	2	..	..	..	..	..	..	..	..	..	..

TABLE No. 17, being Analysis of Cases of Leucorrhœa, Section 3.

Length of time ill.	Cured or greatly bene-fitted.			Some-what bene-fitted.			Un-changed.			Total.	Still under treatment. Greatly bene-fitted.			Some-what bene-fitted.			Un-changed.			Total.	Left treatment too early. Cured or greatly bene-fitted.			Some-what bene-fitted.			Un-changed.			Total.
	Some Leucorrhœa	Cop. Leucorrhœa.	Ocsnl. Leucorrhœa	Some Leucorrhœa.	Cop. Leucorrhœa.	Ocsnl. Leucorrhœa	Some Leucorrhœa	Cop. Leucorrhœa.	Ocsnl. Leucorrhœa		Some Leucorrhœa	Cop. Leucorrhœa.	Ocsnl. Lencorrhœa	Some Leucorrhœa.	Cop. Leucorrhœa.	Ocsnl. leucorrhœa.	Some leucorrhœa.	Cop. leucorrhœa.	Ocsnl. leucorrhœa.		Some leucorrhœa.	Cop. leucorrhœa.	Ocsnl. leucorrhœa.	Some leucorrhœa.	Cop. leucorrhœa.	Ocsnl. leucorrhœa.	Some leucorrhœa.	Cop. leucorrhœa.	Ocsnl. leucorrhœa.	
Under 3 months	2	4	..	..	..	..	..	..	..	6	..	..	..	..	..	..	..	..	..	..	1	..	..	..	..	..	..	..	..	1
.. 6 ..	1	3	..	..	1	..	..	..	..	5	..	..	1	..	..	1	..	..	..	2	..	2	..	..	1	..	..	..	..	3
.. 12 ..	2	8	..	..	..	1	1	1	..	13	2	..	..	..	3	..	..	..	..	5	..	1	1	..	1	..	..	1	..	4
.. 2 years	..	6	2	..	..	1	1	..	..	10	1	1	..	..	..	..	..	..	..	2	1	..	..	1	1	1	..	2	..	6
.. 3 ..	1	3	..	..	..	..	..	2	..	6	..	1	..	..	..	..	..	..	..	1	2	1	..	..	1	..	..	..	..	4
.. 6 ..	..	4	2	..	1	..	..	..	..	7	..	..	1	..	..	..	..	..	..	1	..	2	..	..	..	..	..	..	..	2
Many years	4	3	7	1	2	1	3	4	2	27	..	1	1	..	3	1	..	..	..	6	..	..	..	1	..	1	..	..	..	2
A long time	6	6	..	1	..	1	..	..	..	14	..	..	..	1	..	..	..	..	..	1	..	3	..	1	..	..	..	..	..	4
Unknown	..	1	..	1	..	..	..	..	..	2	..	..	..	..	..	..	..	..	..	..	1	..	..	..	..	..	..	..	..	1

TABLE No. 18, BEING ANALYSIS OF CASES OF LEUCORRHŒA, SECTION 4.

Menstrual functions.	Cured or greatly bene-fitted.			Some-what bene-fitted.			Un-changed.			Total.	Still under treatment.									Total.	Left treatment too early.									Total.
											Greatly bene-fitted.			Some-what bene-fitted.			Un-changed.				Cured or greatly bene-fitted.			Some-what bene-fitted.			Un-changed.			
	Some leucorrhœa.	Cop. leucorrhœa.	Ocsnl. leucorrhœa.	Some leucorrhœa.	Cop. leucorrhœa.	Ocsnl. leucorrhœa.	Some leucorrhœa.	Cop. leucorrhœa.	Ocsnl. leucorrhœa.		Some leucorrhœa.	Cop. leucorrhœa.	Ocsnl. leucorrhœa.	Some leucorrhœa.	Cop. leucorrhœa.	Ocsnl. leucorrhœa.	Some leucorrhœa.	Cop. leucorrhœa.	Ocsnl. leucorrhœa.		Some leucorrhœa.	Cop. leucorrhœa.	Ocsnl. leucorrhœa.	Some leucorrhœa.	Cop. leucorrhœa.	Ocsnl. leucorrhœa.	Some leucorrhœa.	Cop. leucorrhœa.	Ocsnl. leucorrhœa.	
Menses absent......	3	8	1	..	..	1	..	..	..	13	1	..	..	..	1	1	..	..	..	3	1	1	..	1	..	1	..	..	..	4
.. irregular....	1	3	2	1	..	2	..	1	1	11	..	..	..	..	..	..	..	..	..	..	..	..	..	..	1	..	..	..	..	1
.. regular	5	17	1	2	2	..	1	3	..	31	..	..	3	1	2	1	..	..	..	7	1	3	..	1	..	..	..	2	..	7
.. scanty	4	8	1	..	..	..	3	3	1	20	..	..	2	..	2	..	..	..	..	4	..	4	1	..	..	..	..	..	..	5
.. copious	2	10	5	..	2	1	2	3	1	26	1	3	..	1	1	..	..	..	..	6	1	1	..	1	1	..	..	..	..	4
.. too long duration ...	..	..	2	..	..	..	..	..	..	2	..	..	..	..	..	..	..	..	..	..	..	..	..	1	..	..	..	..	..	1
.. painful	3	6	..	..	1	..	1	1	1	13	..	..	1	..	2	1	..	..	..	4	1	2	..	..	1	..	..	..	..	4
.. pale	3	2	1	..	..	..	1	1	..	8	..	..	..	..	1	..	..	..	..	1	..	3	1	..	..	1	..	1	..	6
.. dark	..	4	1	..	..	..	1	1	..	7	..	..	..	..	..	..	..	..	..	..	..	..	..	..	1	..	..	..	..	1
.. too early	1	3	2	1	1	1	1	2	..	11	1	2	..	..	1	..	..	..	..	4	1	2	..	1	..	1	..	..	..	5
.. too late	..	2	1	..	..	1	..	..	..	4	..	..	..	..	1	..	..	..	..	1	2	2	..	..	..	..	..	..	..	4

TABLE No. 19, BEING ANALYSIS OF CASES OF LEUCORRHŒA, SECTION 5.

Length of time under treatment.	Cured or greatly benefitted.			Somewhat benefitted.			Unchanged.			Total.	Still under treatment. Greatly benefitted.			Still under treatment. Somewhat benefitted.			Still under treatment. Unchanged.			Total.	Left treatment too early to judge. Cured or greatly benefitted.			Left treatment too early to judge. Somewhat benefitted.			Left treatment too early to judge. Unchanged.			Total.
	Some leucorrhœa.	Cop. leucorrhœa.	Ocsnl. leucorrhœa.	Some leucorrhœa.	Cop. leucorrhœa.	Ocsnl. leucorrhœa.	Some leucorrhœa.	Cop. leucorrhœa.	Ocsnl. leucorrhœa.		Some leucorrhœa.	Cop. leucorrhœa.	Ocsnl. leucorrhœa.	Some leucorrhœa.	Cop. leucorrhœa.	Ocsnl. leucoarhœa.	Some leucorrhœa.	Cop. leucorrhœa.	Ocsnl. leucorrhœa.		Some leucorrhœa.	Cop. leucorrhœa.	Ocsnl. leucorrhœa.	Some leucorrhœa.	Cop. leucorrhœa.	Ocsnl. leucorrhœa.	Some leucorrhœa.	Cop. leucorrhœa.	Ocsnl. leucorrhœa.	
1 month or less	2	2	..	..	..	..	..	..	..	4	..	..	..	..	2	..	..	..	..	2	2	3	..	..	1	1	..	1	..	8
2	1	9	..	..	..	1	1	..	..	12	..	..	..	..	..	1	..	..	..	1	1	5	..	1	2	..	..	2	..	11
3	..	3	3	..	1	..	1	1	1	10	..	2	2	..	..	..	..	..	..	4	..	..	..	1	1	1	..	..	..	3
4	3	6	..	1	..	1	2	2	..	15	1	..	..	..	..	..	..	..	..	1	1	..	1	..	..	..	..	..	..	2
5	4	4	..	..	..	..	..	..	..	8	1	..	..	..	..	..	..	..	..	1	..	..	..	..	..	..	..	..	..	..
6	1	4	2	1	..	1	..	1	..	10	..	..	..	1	..	..	..	..	..	1	1	1	..	1	..	..	..	..	..	3
9	1	7	1	..	..	..	..	..	..	9	..	..	..	..	1	..	..	..	..	1	..	..	..	..	..	..	..	..	..	..
12	1	..	2	..	..	..	..	2	1	6	..	1	..	..	1	..	..	..	..	2	..	..	..	..	..	..	..	..	..	..
1¼ years	..	1	..	..	2	..	..	..	..	3	1	..	..	..	..	..	..	..	..	1	..	..	..	..	..	..	..	..	..	..
1½ ..	..	..	1	..	..	1	..	..	..	2	..	..	..	..	..	1	..	..	..	1	..	..	..	..	..	..	..	..	..	..
2 or more years	4	1	2	..	1	..	1	..	..	9	..	..	1	..	2	..	..	..	..	3	..	..	..	..	..	..	..	..	..	..
Unknown.	..	1	..	..	..	..	..	..	..	1	..	..	..	..	..	..	..	..	..	..	..	..	..	..	..	..	..	..	..	..

[While we cannot too highly applaud the diligence and zeal displayed by Dr. Madden, in making and recording so many careful examinations of such a multitude of uterine cases, we cannot give a silent assent to the conclusion he arrives at. As the glory of modern surgery is the curing, not the performing of operations, so the excellence of homœopathy ought to be the curing of as many diseases as possible without the use of auxiliary aids, such as local applications, especially caustics, and it is far too soon for any one, however great his experience, to issue a finality bill, and say that such and such diseases can only be cured by surgical operations, unless he can show some better reasons from pathology than his mere inability to find an appropriate remedy, nor, indeed, is this done or intended to be done by Dr. Madden. We must first use all the remedies we have, then look for more; but not till all possible medicinal substances are exhausted, can we confidently assert, here are the limits of internal homœopathic treatment. To assert that nitrate of silver, &c., act specifically as well as chemically, seems to us almost as extravagant as if we were to attribute the benefit of an amputation to the particles of the ferrum absorbed by the cut surface, or to the galvanic or odylic influence in addition to the riddance of the offending member.—EDITORS.]

TABLE No. 20. Condition at the commencement of local treatment of those which were first treated by general remedies.

Somewhat benefitted	11
Unchanged	25

CLINICAL RECORD.

Manchester Homœopathic Hospital.

We find that the number of beds in this institution now amounts to 25, and that from the 29th April to the 15th November, 77 cases have been treated with in general very satisfactory results.

We find that at the same date there were 10 cases in the house.

The fact of this hospital being self supporting and not a free one, may in some measure account for the paucity of acute cases, as in Manchester no one can become an inmate of the establishment without the payment of at least half-a-crown a week, and if without the recommendation of a subscriber the patient is charged five shillings.

This may prove to be a serious drawback to the general usefulness of the Manchester Hospital, and we should fear would always militate against its having that number of acute cases (which are most prevalent amongst the indigent), so essential in the present state of homœopathy in this country, to strike not only the vulgar mind, but also that of the investigating allopathic physician. All who have attempted to influence their allopathic brethren by statements of individual cases, know how these are treated, and how often the "vis medicatrix" is called in to explain away what they have thought to be incontrovertible proofs of the truth of our system.

A Hospital unrestricted in its admissions, except by the opinions of its medical officers, would soon furnish sufficient materials to put the "vis" aside and allopathy also. The self-supporting system is, however, one of those evils under which we must for some time labor, and which can only be got rid of by a wider diffusion of our system amongst the wealthy laity. And in towns where homœopathic hospitals and dispensaries are opened, we would earnestly call upon our brethren to advocate the cause of perfectly free and charitable institutions.

CASE I.—ERYSIPELAS.

April 29th, 1850.—Elizabeth Hynde, admitted to-day, states that on the evening of the 27th she was seized with shivering, and on the 28th the face became swollen and painful, with shooting pains in the head. There is now erysipelatous inflammation of the face, affecting especially the nose, the left cheek, and the upper part of the neck; and the eyelids of both eyes are much swollen. There is severe frontal headache, with subdelirium; the tongue dry and red at the tip and edges.

Belladonna 3d decimal dilution, every two hours.

30th.—She has passed a better night than on either the 27th or 28th. The inflammation has, however, spread to the hairy scalp.

Continue.

May 1st.—Slept well last night; the inflammatory redness and swelling of the face is diminishing; and the swelling of the scalp, though as yesterday, is much less tender. The headache much relieved, and the general febrile symptoms are less. Continue.

May 2d to the 6th.—She has continued to improve. To-day the report is: no appearance of inflammation about face or scalp; desquamation; bowels quite regular; tongue moist; no fever. Sulph. 6.

On the 9th.—Dismissed cured.

CASE II.—FIBROUS TUMOR OF THE UTERUS.

May 1st.—Jane Leatherbarrow, aged 39, married, mother of several children. Eighteen months ago had a miscarriage, since then bloody discharge, very offensive, frequently clottted. The lips, gums, and conjunctiva excessively pale; eyes surrounded with a dark circle; countenance anxious; pulse rapid and feeble; anorexia, nausea, and occasional vomiting; pain and tenderness in the right iliac region; sleepless nights.

Secale 1st decimal dilution. Cocculus 3d ditto, every three hours alternately.

2d.—Less discharge; nausea relieved. Continue.

3d.—Discharge less offensive; pain in the side relieved; general appearance improving.

4th.—Discharge not offensive, scanty, watery. Continue.

From this date to the 14th, the general health continued to improve. Platinum, China, Ipecac., Ferrum, and Secale were prescribed in succession as the symptoms seemed to indicate, and in the interval an examination with the speculum was made, which disclosed a firm tumor protruding from the os uteri.

21st.—A ligature was passed round the neck of the tumor.

Arnica 1.

22d and 23d.—She has suffered considerably from abdominal pain and retention of urine. Bell 2 and Arnica 1, alternately.

26th.—The tumor separated this morning without hemorrhage, it was about 5 inches in length and about 2½ in breadth, lobulated on the surface and somewhat kidney shaped, a section of it displayed its fibrous texture. She left the Hospital on the 10th of June, perfectly well and much improved in flesh and strength.

The above case appears interesting, in so far as it shows the effects of the homœopathic remedies in palliating the symptoms previous to the removal of the tumor by operation, and although the urgency of these would not permit of a longer trial of their action in this case,—in others, less exhausted, might not their continuance lead to a cure?

CASE III.—PLEURO-PNEUMONIA.

May 4th.—John Nicholson, house painter, aged 24; muscular. Cephalalgia; pulse 112; skin burning; tongue moist, with yellow fur, red at the tip; eyes suffused; slight cough; stabbing pain, extending from the point of the right scapula and passing through the chest to the sternum; dry crepitating rattle on the right side of the chest posteriorly. Aconite B, Bryonia B, every two hours alternately.

5th.—Tongue cleaner; breathes with greater freedom: pain confined to a small spot to the right of the right nipple, still felt very acutely on coughing; cough troublesome, with clear thick tenacious sputa; skin moist; pulse 98; crepitating rattle as yesterday; bronchial respiration. Bry. B, Phos. B, every three hours alternately.

6th.—Less pain; more cough; sputa less tenacious; tongue cleaner; pulse 86. Continue.

7th.—Has passed a tolerable night, though much troubled with the cough; sputa yellowish; pain nearly gone.

Continue the Phosphorus alone, and give it at the 3d dilution.

9th.—is doing very well. Crepitus still audible posteriorly.

12th.—States that he feels quite well, and is discharged with a caution to keep quiet for a few days longer. He presented himself a week after, and had entirely got rid of his cough and the slight uneasiness in the chest which he felt at first on taking exercise.

Case IV.

May 29th.—Elizabeth Moorehouse, aged 23, married, and is nursing an infant six months old, complaining for five days. Present symptoms; intense stabbing pain in the left submammary region and lower end of sternum; troublesome short tickling cough; complete dulness in the two lower thirds of the posterior part of the chest, with entire absence of the respiratory murmur; pulse 132.

Aconite B, Bryonia B, every two hours alternately.

30th.—Still intense pain in left side, stabbing in character; skin moist; pulse 128. Bry. B, Phos. B, every two hours alternately.

31st.—Pulse 110; pain less stabbing in character; rather less dulness on percussion, but the respiratory murmur is inaudible.

Bry. 3, Phos. 3, every three hours alternately.

June 1st.—Pulse 96; less pain; respiratory murmur slightly audible. Continue.

2d.—Pulse 86; very little pain, and its character is now dull; more resonance; murmur more distinct. Continue.

4th.—No pain; very slight dulness; the left side expands on deep inspiration.

6th.—Respiration tolerably free, and the respiratory murmur is quite distinct; some dulness remains; she complains of nothing but weakness, and calls loudly for meat.

China A, T. Sulph. φ, every four hours alternately.

10th.—She is dressed, states that she is quite well; the chest not examined, but as she breathed freely, had no pain or cough, and complained of nothing but the still too scanty diet, she was dismissed with directions to take a powder containing one drop of T. Sulph. φ, each night for a week longer.

Cases like the above have occurred to every practitioner of homœopathy, but are particularly interesting to those who have treated similar cases on the old plan. What a contrast does the noble simplicity of our treatment present in its administration of a few remedies, and these apparently inert to the labored complexness of the V. S. the Cucurb. Cruent., the leeches, the blisters, and last, but most dangerous, the Calomel and Opium, (to ptyalism sometimes, in a strumous subject!) In this aspect did it present itself to a young physician, who saw and watched the case of Elizabeth Moorehouse, and from what he did see he concluded that homœopathy was worthy of his serious attention. Since then he has been steadily studying and is now a zealous convert.

CASE V.—ACUTE PLEURISY.

July 4th.—Riley Thomas, aged 18, single, laborer, was visited at his own home, and had the following symptoms, at 11 A. M. Acute pain in the right side, striking like a knife running into him, as he said, at every breath; his hand was pressed upon the side to restrain the motions of the chest; breathing abdominal; great inclination to cough, but restrained as much as possible from the violent pain which the effort brought on; there was some dulness over the part, and upon applying the stethescope distinct friction sound was heard; pain acute on pressing upon the intercostal spaces; had had rigors; pulse 104, full and hard; skin hot and dry; tongue furred; countenance anxious; great thirst; urine scanty and high-colored; bowels relaxed from Sulphate of Magnesia.

Take Acon. B. Bry. 3, every hour alternataly.

7 P. M.—Found him much relieved. Pulse 98; could breathe comparatively freely; cough with very little pain; skin moist; thirst not so urgent; countenance much more tranquil.

Continue every two hours.

5th, 9 A. M.—Was removed in a car carefully enveloped in blankets to the hospital.

2 P. M.—Symptoms aggravated in consequence of his removal. Fever increased; pain in side worse; tongue dry; diarrhœa has set in.

Acon. 3, Ars. 6, every two hours alternately.

6th.—Slept tolerably well during the night; cough troublesome; still pain in right side; no diarrhœa; tongue cleaner and moist; pulse 88, weak; some dulness on percussion, no friction sound.

Continue Acon. occasionally, Merc. 1, Chin. A.

7th—Much better this morning. Skin moist; tongue cleaner; bowels acted naturally last night; pulse 84, soft and regular; slight pain in right side; cough easier, with mucous expectoration.

Continue.

8th—Very much better, all pain gone. Cough very slight.

Continue.

9th.—Reports himself well and was discharged this day.

Case VI.—Rheumatism.

Aug. 16th, 1850.—Martin Corrigan, aged 51, laborer, married, admitted into hospital to-day. Has been exposed to cold and wet. Complains of pains in the back and lower extremities of a shooting character, with a sense of contraction in the tendons of the thigh; urine scanty and high colored; bowels sluggish; he feels worse in a morning.

Take Bry. B, Puls. 3, every two hours alternately.

17th.—Rather better. Continue.

18th.—Much better. Complains now of pains chiefly in the knees; perspiring freely. Continue.

20th.—Better.

Take Bry. B, Arn. B, every three hours alternately.

Continued improving up to 23d, when he was discharged cured.

Case VII.

Nov. 15th.—Margaret Hobbs, aged 26, married, came to the hospital as an out-patient. Has been subject to rheumatism. Complains now of pains in the joints of upper and lower extremities, more particularly of the ankle-joints and feet; is cold and chilly; thirst; pulse accelerated; tongue furred; bowels constipated; urine scanty and high-colored.

Take Acon. B, Bell. B, every two hours alternately.

16th.—Was visited at her own home. All the symptoms were much aggravated. She was sitting close by the fire, and still cold; pulse 100 and jerking; tongue much furred, dry, red tip and edges; face flushed, skin dry; pains in the limbs very acute; ankles and feet swollen, hot and painful to the touch; she dreaded night approaching, the pains were so violent when warm in bed, and prevented her sleeping. She was ordered to continue her medicine, and to come into hospital the following day.

17th.—Admitted into hospital. Somewhat better, still pains acute and ankle-joints and feet still swollen, hot, and painful to the touch; she is unable to walk; bowels have acted; pulse 104, compressible.

Take Bell. B, Rhus B, every two hours alternately.

19th.—Feels better; has had a better night; pain almost gone from the right ankle-joint. Continue.

20th.—Pains almost gone; legs continue swollen. Continue.

23d.—Feels quite well, with the exception of some debility. Discharged cured.

Case VIII.

Sept. 2d.—John Mews, aged 38, married, admitted into hospital. States that he has been ill for thirteen months. After unusual exestion he was seized with pain in stomach, and in the shoulders, armr, back and lower extremities; the pains have recently become much worse, and he cannot now raise the right arm; great pain in right shoulder, between the scapulæ and down the back; pain and stiffness of the right knee, left leg and foot also very painful, with stiffness of the heel; left foot very hot; bowels regular; tongue coated and brown; skin hot and dry; pulse accelerated.

Take Bry. 3, Rhus 3, every three hours alternately.

3d.—Same. Continue.

5th.—A little better. Tongue clean; bowels relieved.

Ordered a warm bath, and Ars. B, Bry. 3, every four hours alternately.

6th.—Same. Perspired freely in the night after the bath; bowels relieved; urine high colored, depositing a thick white sediment.

Continue.

7th.— Profuse nightly perspiration affording no relief; skin hot; bowels relieved; tongue coated; on examining the heart with the stethoscope a distinct bruit is heard; action accelerated but feeble; starts from his sleep with violent palpitation; increased dulness in the præcordial region.

Continue, Arsen. B, Bry. 3, every four hours alternately.

8th.—Same. Continue.

9th.—Same. Continue.

10th.—Pulse 84; heart sounds more distinct.

11th.—Same. Take Arsen. B, Digit. B, every four hours alternately.

12th and 13th.—Unable still to raise right arm.

14th.—Same. Continue.

15th.—Better. Heart sounds more distinct, with bruit at apex. Continue.

16th.—Tingling in right arm. Continue.

17th.—Same.

18th.—Heart's action more distinct, and bruit not so marked; considerable pain in right shoulder. Continue.

20th.—Same.

21st.—Better to day. Heart sounds normal; pains much better; leg and arm of right side continue a little stiff.

Continue Digit. B., Arsen. B.

22d.—Discharged at his own request, as he states that he feels nearly well.

Case IX.

June 5th.—John Hindley, aged 26, miner. Several months ago was seized with dull aching pain in the region of the kidneys, which was followed with anasarcous swelling, commencing at the face and gradually extended over the body to the lower extremities, and which continues: legs, feet, and abdomen are now much swollen, tongue coated with a yellow fur; pulse rapid and feeble; bowels regular; urine scanty and pale, with a greenish tinge.

Digit. 3, Ars. 3, every three hours alternately.

7th.—General health better; on examination, the urine was found highly albuminous. Continue.

8th.—Less swollen. Continue.

9th, 10th and 11th.—Swelling diminishing; urine sp. gr. 10.12. Continue.

12th.—Urine, 10.14. Continue.

13th.—Urine, 10.18. Continue.

15th.—Swelling very much reduced. Continue.

July 2d.—Swelling has entirely disappeared, although the urine still contains traces of albumen, and he left the hospital for the benefit of sea-side air.

In this case but two medicines were given, Digit. and Ars., and the effect was to remove completely the dropsical affection in less than a month. Previous to his admission into hospital he had for two months been under allopathic treatment, at one of the Manchester dispensaries, without receiving any relief, although the most potent diuretics, and amongst the rest Digitalis had been unsparingly administered.

Case X.—Continued Fever.

June 4th—J. Matthews, M.D. Febrile symptoms; great pain in head; bowels confined for several days; pulse 140. Acon. 3, Bell. 3, Bry. 3.

5th.—Tongue coated yellow; great heat and pain in head; bowels acted upon; pulse better; debility. Ars. B, Bell. 3

6th.—Less fever; less thirst; still bitter taste in mouth; tongue less coated; pulse better; feels better, though week. Continue.

7th.—Slept better last night; symptoms much improved; tongue cleaning; pulse increasing; bowels acted upon last night.

Ars. B, and Bry.

8th.—Same. Continue.

9th.—Delirium this morning about 5 o'clock, threatened to get out of bed; wishes to go out; pulse 94, small; tongue moist and cleaner; forehead cool; debility much. Bell. 3, Ars. B, and Stram. 3. 3 P. M. —Great excitement; talks continuously of going home. Stram. 3, Bell. 3. Half-past 7 P. M.—Found him up and partially dressed, expressing a determination to go home; was eventually prevailed on with much persuasion to return to bed. Acon. 3, Ars. B, and Bell 3, *si opus sit.* Quarter past 9 P. M.—Less excitement, but very restless; skin hot; pulse 94, full; occasional muttering delirium. 10 P. M.—More tranquil; inclined to dose. Bell 3, Ars. 3.

10th, three quarters past 8 P. M.—Passed a pretty tranquil night, was rather excited about 3 o'clock this morning, got up and wanted to go away; he is now tranquil; pulse 94, small; tongue very dry; skin hot; bowels were opened yesterday afternoon. Continue.

11th.—Slept well until about half-past 4 o'clock this morning, when he got up and wanted to go down stairs, he said, for his clothes; the nurse with some difficulty got him into bed again, when he became quiet and remained so till this morning at 9 o'clock; pulse 86; tongue moist; skin rather cool and moist; tongue coated yellow; bowels regular; is rather inclined to ramble, but on the whole much more rational than yesterday. Continue Acon. 3.

12th.—Slept well last night; skin moist; tongue moist and cleaner; bowels acted upon last night; no rambling, is quiet. Continue.

13th.—Slept well last night until about 8 o'clock this morning, when he asked for his clothes, and desired the nurse to procure a cab as he wished to go home; seems easier now; not much fever; bowels regular. Continue Ars. 3.

14th.—Had a very good night's rest; skin cool and moist; tongue moist and much cleaner; is much better in every respect. Continue.

15th.—Slept very comfortably last night; skin cool and moist; tongue cleaning; perfectly rational; bowels acted naturally this morning. Continue.

16th.—Much better. China 1, Bell. 3.

17th.—Convalescent. Continue.

MANCHESTER HOMŒOPATHIC HOSPITAL.

Disease.	Age.	Whether under old treatment.	How long ill.	How long under treatment.	Event.	Chief medicines used.
1 Anasarca	26	yes	several weeks	1 month	cured	Dig. B, Ars. 6
2 Abscess on left thigh	17	yes	6 months	6 weeks	cured	Nux B; Bell. B, Graph. 5
3 Ascites..................	49			2 weeks		
4 Bronchitis	31	yes		2 weeks	cured	Acon. 3, Bry. 3, Phos. 3, Nux 3, Hyos. 1
5 Bronchitis chronica	25	yes		5 days (discharged for disobedience)	much relieved	Merc. 3, Rhus 3
6 Cancerous mamma	45	yes	2 years	3 weeks	cured	Con. 1, Nux B
7 Chlorosis	24	yes	4 months	1 month	cured	Puls. 3, Ars. 6, Bell. 6, Sulph. 12
8 Catarrhal fever	25	no	3 weaks	3 weeks	cured	Bell. B, Acon. B, Nux B
9 Cephalalgia						
10 Caries, ankle joint amputated	15	yes	9 months	7 weeks (amputated)	cured	Arn. A, Bell. B, Acon. B, Merc. 3
11 Delirium tremens	23	no		5 days	cured	Nux B
12 Diarrhœa chronica	43	yes	3 years	3 weeks	cured	Camph. O, Arsenic. 6
13 Dysuria	43			3 weeks	much relieved	Canth. 1, Sep., Sulph., Carb. veg.
14 Epilepsy	28	yes	14 years	1 week		Calc. 12, Nux B, Bell. B, Hyos. B
15 Erysipelas						
16 Epilepsy	26	yes	4 years	3 weeks	much relieved	Bell. B, Nux Op.
17 Erysipelas, facial					cured	Bell.
18 Epilepsy	11	yes		2 weeks	relieved	Bell. 3, Op. 1, Acon. B
19 Epilepsy	34	yes	11 years	in hospital		
20 Erysipelas, facial						Hell. O, Phos. 3, Hyos. 1, Merc.
21 Erysipelas, facial	29	no	2 or 3 weeks	1 week	cured	Bell. B, Acon. B, Merc. 3, Petiv.
22 Fistula lachrymalis	30	yes		2 weeks	cured	Merc. 3, Hep. 6, Sil. 12
23 Fistula in ano	45	yes	4 years	2 months		Acon. 1, Sulph. O, Hep. s. B
24 Gastralgia	34	yes		5 weeks	much relieved	Hyos. A, Nux, Puls., Sulph. 12
25 Gastralgia, hysteria	26			2 weeks	much relieved	Bell. B, Bry. B, Ignat. B, Nux B
26 Gastralgia	23					Nux B, Puls. B, China 1, Bell.
27 Hysteria	38	yes	4 years	7 weeks	much relieved	Ign. B, Nux 3, Cocc. 3, Merc. 1

No.	Disease	Age					Remedies
28	Hepatitis, chronic	76	yes	14 months	2 months	much relieved	Nux, Dig., Bry. B, Merc. B
29	Hemiplegia	59	yes	4 months	5 weeks	cured	Nux, Acon., Bry. B, Sab. B
30	Lateral curvature of spine	17	yes	several years	5 weeks	much relieved	Teu. B, Iod. B, Bell. B
31	Lumbago	53			3 weeks	much relieved	Cann. 1, China 1
32	Morbus coxarius	8	yes	9 months	2 months	much relieved	Sil. 6, Calc. 3
33	Mania	25			1 day		
34	Ophthalmia purulenta	35	yes		10 days	much relieved	Cann., Merc. 3, Con.
35	Phthisis pulmonalis	54	yes	9 months	2 weeks	cured	Phos. B, Ars. B, Hyos., Bell.
36	Psoas Abscess	38	yes		3 weeks	cured	Acon. B, Bell., Hep. s. 3
37	Pneumonia chronica?	16	yes	6 months	5 weeks	relieved	Phos. 3, Hep. s. 3, T. Sulph. O
38	Pneumonia						
39	Phthisis pulmonalis	20			2 weeks		Ol. Jecoris Ass., Phos.
40	Pleurisy	18		1 week	5 days	cured	Acon. 3, Rhus., Bry. 6
41	Pyrosis	33	yes	2 years	3 weeks	much relieved	Bry. 3, Bell. 3, Arg. nit. 1, Nux 15
42	Phthisis pulmonalis	18	yes		3 days		Ars. B, China 3, Bry. B
43	Phthisis	22	yes		3 weeks	cured	Ars. 3, Bry. 3, Phos. 3, Ol. Jecoris Ass., Sulph.
44	Rheumatism, chronic	27	yes	3 years	3 weeks	much relieved	Bry. B, Rhus B
45	Rheumatism, chronic	51	yes		1 week	much relieved	Bry. B, Puls. B, Arn. B
46	Rheumatism, acute	25			3 weeks	cured	Ars. B, Bry. B
47	Rheumatism	38	yes	13 months	3 weeks	much relieved	Bry. B, Ars. B, Dig. B
48	Rheumatism, chronic	21	yes		2 weeks	cured	Acon. 3, Rhus, Bry. 6
49	Rheumatism, chronic	42	yes	11 weeks	3 weeks		Bell. B, Bry. B, Rhus B, Sil. 3
50	Rheumatism, chronic	55	yes		3 weeks	cured	Bry., Rhus 3, Sulph., Ol. Jecoris Ass.
51	Rheumatism, acute	51	yes		1 week	much relieved	Bry. B., Puls. B., Acon. B
52	Syphilitic lepra	43	yes	6 months			Sep. 3, Puls. 3
53	Struma of great toe	24	yes	10 months	1 week		Sil. B
54	Struma of elbow joint	16	yes	3 years	2 weeks		Ars. 6, Hep. s. 3
55	Synovitis	57	yes	several weeks	in hospital		
56	Synovitis chronica	39	yes	3 months	2 weeks	cured	Sil. 12
57	Synovitis chronica	17	yes	11 months		much relieved	Calc. 3, Bry. B
58	Syphilitic rheumatism	24	yes		5 weeks	cured	Merc. 3, Rhus 1, Nit. ac. B, Calc. c.
59	Subacute pleuritis	29			3 weeks	cured	Merc. B, Bry. B, Acon. B, Bell. B
60	Typhus fever						
61	Ulcers	24	yes	9 months	6 weeks	cured	Lach. 6, Sil. 12, Puls. 3
62	Ulcer	45			still in hosp.		
63	Uterine tumor	39	yes	18 months	2 weeks	cured	Sec. 1, Cocc., Plat. 6, Phos.

THE HAHNEMANN HOSPITAL.

This hospital has been in full operation since the 16th of October. We subjoin a short abstract of the cases that have been received in-doors. The number of out-patients treated up to this date (December 18th) is above 650.

No.	Sex.	Age.	Condition.	Disease.	Duration of disease before admission	Date of admission.	Date of Discharge.	Result.	Chief Medicines given.	REMARKS.
1	M	13	S	typhus fever	5 days	Oct. 18	Oct. 30	cured	ars. 3, bell. 3, bry. 3	Not a very severe case; delirious for four nights after admission.
2	M	40	M	hypertrophy of the heart, with fever	10 months	Oct. 23	Nov. 25	greatly improved	rhus. 3, nux vom.2, bry. 3, spig. 2, merc. 30, cocc. 12, aur. 12	For ten months he had been in allopathic hospitals and dispensaries; amongst the medicines he took were strychnine, sesqui-carbonate of iron, vinum antimonii, æther nitricus, acidum sulphuris, &c., without any relief: for the last five months he had every second day castor oil, to relieve his costiveness. The palpitation of the heart and even the bellows sound is greatly diminished, as well as a particular squeezing feeling on the right side of the chest. He is still improving since he left the hospital, as reported on the 14th December by his wife. The disease began probably after rheumatism of the legs.
3	M	28	S	rheumatic fever	2 weeks	Oct. 31	Nov. 9	cured	bry. 2, bry. 12	Till the day before his admission under allopathic treatment. The pains and swellings of both his hands and arms, which hindered the movement of these parts, disappeared the sixth day.
4	M	17	S	violent rheumatic fever	2 weeks	Oct. 31	Still in hospital	cured	bry. 12, rhus 12, bry. 3, merc. 30, colch.3, chin. 5, rhus 12	The patient came very emaciated, and looking very pale, to the hospital; almost all the articulations, and even the bowels, were very painful. On the 15th November he was without medicine, and allowed to get up, as he had no complaint; the following night he had a

										return of his disease in a less violent degree, and the last few days he is again up for some hours at a time; it is more for his general strength that he is still in the hospital.
5	M	18	S	orchitis from suppressed gonorrhœa	gonorrhœa a month since, orchitis 4 days	Nov. 2	Dec. 2	cured	acon. & puls., clem., cann., nux, canth., merc., sulph.	Aconite, Puls. and Clematis for the acute stage of orchitis; Cannabis, Merc. and Sulph. for the gonorrhœa, and Nux for dyspeptic symptoms. The gonorrhœa was not cured.
6	F	13	S	cardiac disease and rheumatism	6 months	Nov. 10	Nov. 21	much better	spig. 3, bry. 3, bell. 3	Loud bruit with heart's first sound, and great pain in the heart and limbs; the pains were quite removed by the treatment.
7	F	17	S	morbis coxarius	2 years	Nov. 11	still in hospital	improved	silic., puls., calc., merc., phos.	Has two abscesses on the left hip, one on the left vulva, and one on the upper third of the right humerus; the Mercurius lessened the night sweats and improved the condition of the pus.
8	F	20	S	irregular and suppressed menstruation; swollen legs	irregular for 5 years, suppressed for 6 weeks	Nov. 14	Dec. 2	cured	puls., sulph., nux, bry. and calc.	
9	F	21	S	pleurodynia	3 weeks	Nov. 14	Nov. 23	cured	bry. 3, arn. 3, nux v. 4	The pains were so violent, and accompanied by fever, that the disease was very similar to an inflammatory state. Since the 21st Nov. she was without medicine.
10	M	10	S	bronchitis, acute	3 days	Nov. 14	Nov. 22	cured	bry. 3, puls. 3	A very scrofulous subject; much concomitant gastric derangement.
11	M	45	M	diarrhœa	3 days	Nov. 15	Nov. 18	cured	nux 3, ars. 6	Affected besides with chronic dyspnœa, which was not treated.
12	M	47	M	typhus fever	5 days	Nov. 19	Nov. 22	died	ars. 3, bry. 3, bell. 3, op. 3, tart. em. 3	Very much addicted to drinking; the fever was complicated with delirium tremens and nearly total suppression of urine. He died quite suddenly in convulsions.
13	F	35	M	typhus fever	10 days	Nov. 19	still in hospital	convalescent	ars. 3, bry. 3, bell. 3, carb-v. 5, merc. 5, stram. 3	This case presented very bad symptoms: almost uninterrupted delirium for the first ten days, mouth covered with black sordes, tongue hard, black, dry. After the delirium left, was very weak. Is now almost well.
14	F	10	S	typhus fever	4 days	Nov. 19	still in hospital	cured	bry., nux v., chin.	Is only in the hospital for weakness.

No.	Sex.	Age.	Condition.	Disease.	Duration of disease before admission	Date of Admission.	Date of Discharge.	Result.	Chief Medicines given.	REMARKS.
15	M	17	S	bronchitis and hypertrophhy of the heart	1 month 4 years	Nov. 23	Dec. 72	cured and improved	acon. 3, bry. 3, calc. 12, puls. 30, aur. 12, china 30	The 29th November, the tenth day, the bronchitis was cured. The three last medicines were administered for the heart disease; he was obliged to sit up in the bed when he entered the hospital—when he left he preferred to lie almost without a pillow. The disease of the heart originated from a rheumatic fever four years ago for which he was treated.
16	F	24	S	chr. metritis gast. ent. general debility	14 days	Nov. 23	Still in hospital	—	acon. 3, arsen. 3, puls. china	
17	F	27	M	gastr. enteritis	4 days	Dec. 2	Dec. 11	convalescent	acon. 3, arsen. 3, puls. 3, bryon. 3	
18	F	7	—	gastric fever and diarrhœa	2 months	Dec. 2	Dec. 10	cured	bry. 3, ipec. 3, china 3	This child suffered, in consequence of aperient medicines, for two months from diarrhœa 7—8 times a day; she was very emaciated, the abdomen tympanitic, the pulse extremely weak, and deaf for some days before her admission. These details were reported by the mother only the second day, and then only she got *ipecacuanha*, on which she became better; the eighth day her deafness began to diminish suddenly, after having slept a great deal. *China* was given only after she got up the first time from her bed.
19	F	32	S	bronchitis	3 weeks	Dec. 2	Dec. 15	much improved	nux 3, ars. 3	Great dyspnœa and much viscid expectoration, could not lie down at night; these symptoms were nearly removed and the acute attack cured, but there remained chronic bronchitis, to which she had long been subject.

20	F	35	Wid.	chronic bronchitis	for years; the present attack for some months	Dec. 3	Dec. 13	slightly improved	acon. & bry., merc. phos., calc. c.	Was relieved of pain in the chest, and cough, but remained in a sinking state, and left the hospital of her own accord.
21	F	13	S	anœmia	1 year	Dec. 3	Dec. 13	improved	ferr. & china	Left the hospital of her own accord.
22	F	22	S	bronchial irritation.	2 weeks	Dec. 4	in the hospital	cured	bry. 3, nux 5, ipec. 3	
23	M	32	S	dislocation of the sternal end of right clavicle	3 days	Dec. 11	still in hospital	—	arnica, rhus.	
24	M	20	S	disease of brain, inducing delirium.	6 months	Dec. 1	in hospital	improved	acon., . bell., bry., nux	The fit of delirium did not come on, although the premonitory signs were present. Bry. and Nux given for gastric symptoms. Mother subject to epilepsy before his birth.
25	F	22	S	gastro-enteritis	7 days	Dec. 15	still in hospital	convalescent	nux vom. 6	
26	F	3	S	bronchitis	5 days	Dec. 15	still in hospital	convalescent	acon. 3, bry. 3	

WM. RADDE,

PUBLISHER, 322 BROADWAY, N. Y.

HOMŒOPATHIC MEDICINES.

Wm. Radde, 322 Broadway, New-York, respectfully informs the Homœopathic Physicians, and the friends of the System, that he is the sole Agent for the Leipzig Central Homœopathic Pharmacy, and that he has always on hand a good assortment of the best Homœopathic Medicines, in complete sets or by single vials, in *Tinctures, Dilutions* and *Triturations;* also *Pocket Cases of Medicines; Physicians' and Family Medicine Chests to Laurie's Domestic* (60 to 82 Remedies)—EPP'S (60 Remedies)—HERING'S (82 to 90 Remedies)—*Small Pocket Cases*, at $3, with Family Guide and 27 Remedies.—*Cases* containing 415 Vials with Tinctures and Triturations for Physicians.—*Cases* with 260 Vials of Tinctures and Triturations to Jahr's New Manual, or Symtomen-Codex.—Physician's *Pocket Cases* with 60 Vials of Tinctures and Triturations.—*Cases* from 200 to 300 Vials with low and high dilutions of medicated pellets.—*Cases* from 50 to 80 Vials of low and high dilutions, etc., etc. Homœopathic Chocolate. Refined Sugar of Milk, pure Globules, etc. *Arnica Tincture*, the best specific remedy for bruises, sprains, wounds, etc. *Arnica Plaster*, the best application for *Corns. Urtica urens*, the best specific remedy for *Burns.* Also, Books, Pamphlets, and Standard Works on the System, in the English, French, and German languages.

HOMŒOPATHIC BOOKS.

JUST PUBLISHED:

The North American Homœopathic Journal will be published by the subscriber quarterly, on the first days of *February, May, August and November.* It will contain one hundred and forty-four pages, and will be conducted by Dr. Constantine Hering, of Philadelphia, and Drs. E. E. Marcy and J. W. Metcalf, of New-York.

The British Journal of Homœopathy, and the **North American** Homœopathic Journal, will be furnished to subscribers at Five Dollars a year for both; or they may be had separately.

Terms: Three Dollars *per annum*, payable on delivery of the first number. Subscriptions to be directed to W. RADDE, No. 322 Broadway, New-York.

Laurie, Dr. J., Homœopathic Domestic Medicine, with the Treatment and Diseases of Females, Infants, Children, and Adults. 5th American edition. much enlarged, with additions by A. Gerald Hull, M. D. 1850. Bound, $1 50.

Laurie, Dr. J., Elements of Homœopathic Practice of Physic. An Appendix to Laurie's Domestic, containing also all the Diseases of the URINARY AND GENITAL ORGANS. Bound, 1849. $1 25.

C. Hering's Domestic Physician. Fifth American edition, revised, with additions from the author's manuscript of the seventh German edition. 1851. $2.

Ed. C. Chepmell's Domestic Homœopathy restricted to its legitimate sphere of practice, together with rules for diet and regimen. First American edition, with additions and improvements by Samuel B. Barlow, M. D. 1849. Bound, 50 cts.

Laurie's Homœopathic Domestic, by A. Gerald Hull, M. D. Small edition. Bound. 1849. 50 cts.

Hempel's Boenninghausen, for Homœopathic Physicians; to be used at the Bedside of the Patient, and in studying the Materia Medica Pura. 1 octavo vol., most complete edition, including the Concordances of Homœopathic Remedies. Translated and adapted to the use of the American profession, by C. J. Hempel, M. D. 1847. $1 50.

Jahr's New Manual of Homœopathic Practice; Edited, with Annotations, by A. Gerald Hull, M. D. From the last Paris edition. This is the fourth American edition of a very celebrated work, written in French by the eminent Homœopathic Professor Jahr, and it is considered the best practical compendium of this extraordinary science that has yet been composed. After a very judicious and instructive introduction, the work presents a table of the Homœopathic Medicines, with their names in Latin, English, and German; the order in which they are to be studied, with their most important distinctions, and clinical illustrations of their symptoms and effects upon the various organs and functions of the human system. The second volume embraces an elaborate Analysis of the indications in disease, of the medicines adapted to cure, and a Glossary of the technics used in the work, arranged so luminously as to form an admirable guide to every medical student. The whole system is here displayed with a modesty of pretension, and a scrupulosity in statement, well calculated to bespeak candid investigation. This laborious work is indispensable to the students and practitioners of Homœopathy, and highly interesting to medical and scientific men of all classes. Symptomatology and Repertory complete in 2 vols., bound, $6.

Jahr's New Manual; originally published under the name of Symptomen-Codex. (Digest of Symptoms.) This work is intended to facilitate a comparison of the parallel symptoms of the various Homœopathic agents, thereby enabling the practitioner to discover the characteristic symptoms of each drug, and to determine with ease and correctness what remedy is most Homœopathic to the existing group of symptoms. Translated, with important and extensive additions from various sources, by Charles Julius Hempel, M. D., assisted by James M. Quin, M. D., with revisions and clinical notes by John F. Gray, M. D.; contributions by Drs. A. Gerald Hull, B. F. Joslin, and George W. Cook, of New-York; and Drs. C. Hering, J. Jeanes, C. Neidhard, W. Williamson, and J. Kitchen of Philadelphia; with a preface by Constantine Hering, M. D., 2 vols. Bound, 1848. $11.

www.ingramcontent.com/pod-product-compliance
Lightning Source LLC
LaVergne TN
LVHW021428110826
845150LV00007B/2132